The
PILGRIM'S
STORY

The Life & Spirituality of St Ignatius Loyola

Brendan Comerford SJ

Published by Messenger Publications, 2017

ISBN 978 1 910248 39 3

Designed by Messenger Publications Design Department
Typeset in Times New Roman
Printed by Johnswood Press Ltd.

Messenger Publications,
37 Lower Leeson Street, Dublin D02 W938
www.messenger.ie

Contents

PART 1

The Life of St Ignatius Loyola

PART 2

The Spirituality of St Ignatius Loyola

Preface

As the title suggests, this book sets out to be an introduction to the life and spirituality of St Ignatius Loyola. It is not intended for those who are already familiar with St Ignatius's life or for specialists in Ignatian spirituality. My intention here is more pastoral than academic. I had in mind anyone desiring some general, informed knowledge about this influential saint and his spirituality. My hope is that this book will help anyone who desires to find God in daily life, after the manner of Ignatius.

Having just written that this book is not intended for the Ignatian specialist, the general reader may wonder about the presence of so many endnotes in the text. There's no need for concern! These notes are intended to provide some additional information to anyone interested in the many characters and events referred to, but they can be safely bypassed if the reader so chooses.

The title of the book reflects Ignatius's own description of himself as a pilgrim. Following his conversion in Loyola, his life was indeed a sort of pilgrimage for many years, as he moved from one place to another. In a still deeper sense, however, he was a pilgrim to the end of his life, always in search of a way to God. Indeed, that is the description given to the Society of Jesus in one of its founding documents, the *Formula of the Institute*. In describing the Ignatian approach as 'a way to God', Ignatius and his early companions were proclaiming it as one way among many, for there are indeed many ways to God – Benedictine, Franciscan, Dominican, Carmelite and many more – all with their distinctive and helpful characteristics. The Ignatian way is one among them.

This book is divided almost equally into two parts, the first half treating of the life of Ignatius and the second dealing specifically with his spirituality. The bibliography is added for those readers who may wish to delve further into the subject.

May you, the reader, profit from reading these pages. May you be helped to reflect at a deeper level, and to grow in the felt knowledge, love and service of God and your neighbour, as Ignatius would wish. All to the greater glory of God.

Brendan Comerford SJ

PART 1

The Life of St Ignatius Loyola

CHAPTER 1

The World of Ignatius

Ignatius Loyola (1491–1556) lived in interesting times. In the year of his birth, Granada, the last Muslim stronghold in Spain, fell to the armies of King Ferdinand and Queen Isabella. This momentous event put an end to 800 years of Muslim occupation in Spain. Muslim religious books were burnt, except for those dealing with science or philosophy, which were considered to be especially useful. These latter books were transferred to the University of Alcalá de Henares, situated thirty-five kilometers north of Madrid. Most committed Muslims crossed peacefully to North Africa; others converted to Christianity, at least in name, in order to hold on to their property.

In August 1492, Christopher Columbus set sail for the New World, his voyage culminating in the discovery of the Americas, thus opening up a whole new world and vast wealth, especially for Spain.

1492 was also the year that a Spaniard, Rodrigo Borgia, was elected pope, taking the name Alexander VI. He became famous in his own lifetime for his not-so-papal lifestyle – more recently, his reputation has been brought to our television screens in the series *The Borgias*.

1497 saw Vasco da Gama sail around the Cape of Good Hope, a voyage that would later have particular significance for Jesuit missionaries on their way to the Indies and even further afield.

The early decades of the sixteenth century brought such historically important figures onto the European stage as Girolamo Savonarola,

Desiderius Erasmus, Martin Luther, Michelangelo, John Calvin, Henry VIII, Thomas More and El Greco. The list could continue. When describing the sixteenth century, perhaps we could borrow from the opening lines of Charles Dickens's novel, *A Tale of Two Cities*: 'It was the best of times, it was the worst of times, it was the age of wisdom, it was the age of foolishness, it was the epoch of belief, it was the epoch of incredulity, it was the season of Light, it was the season of Darkness, it was the spring of hope, it was the winter of despair.'

The Early Years

In 1491 Iñigo – or Eñico – López de Loyola was born in the ancestral home of the Loyola family, in the parish of Azpeitia in the Basque province of Guipúzcoa in northern Spain. Iñigo was a popular name in that region, after the saintly abbot of the town of Oña near Burgos. Iñigo was the youngest of thirteen children.[1] His parents had been married twenty-four years when he was born.

Beltrán, Ignatius's father, fought for King Ferdinand and Queen Isabella of Spain in a war against the King of Portugal. In acknowledgement of his services, Beltrán was awarded the patronage of the church of Azpeitia by royal charter, dated 10 June 1484. This gave Beltrán almost the same powers as those of a local bishop: he could present nominees for the office of parish priest, appoint two chaplains, occupy the seat of honour in the church, and select a place there for his own tomb where he might rest for eternity.

Two of Beltrán's children, Juan and Maria, were illegitimate. Local records of the time reveal that Beltrán signed his last will and testament on 23 October 1507, and he is thought to have died the same day. Ignatius would have been sixteen years old at the time.

Ignatius's mother, Marina Sánchez de Licona, was the daughter of Doctor Martín de Licona, auditor of the High Court of Justice; he had considerable influence in the court of Castile. His brother, Juan Pérez de Licona, founded the first monastery of the reformed Franciscans in Guipúzcoa. Marina's marriage contract with Beltrán is dated 13 July 1467. The date of her death is unknown. It may well have been soon after Ignatius's birth; it was certainly before 1498, when her eldest surviving son, Martín García, married Doña Magdalena de Aroaz and became Lord of Loyola. Marina's eldest son, Juan Peréz, had equipped his own ship and taken part in the wars against France for the possession of Naples, where he died of his wounds in battle.

The Loyola coat of arms, seen still today over the entrance to the castle of Loyola, was a camp kettle or cauldron hung by a chain between two wolves. The kettle is said to suggest that after generous feasting there was always something left for the wolves. The *lobo* (wolf) and the *olla* (pot) evoke by the sound of their syllables the word *Loyola*. As a place name, Loyola, meaning a muddy site, was common to several regions of the Basque country. It was not exactly a complimentary description of the land.

The Loyolas were eminent among the *ricos hombres* of the province. The word *ricos* indicated a ruling class rather than a rich one. As the youngest son, Ignatius would be landless and he therefore belonged to the second degree of nobility, or *hidalgos*, men distinguished by their noble lineage.

A few days after his birth, Ignatius was handed over to a wet nurse, María de Guerin, wife of a local blacksmith. María lived in a cottage not far from the castle of Loyola. It was a normal practice among the upper classes in Europe, well into the eighteenth century, for a newborn baby to be handed over to a local wet nurse, with infants placed in the care of a village woman for one or two years. It was a common belief that a mother's milk was spoilt by sexual intercourse, which most couples were unwilling to forgo for such a long period.

Almost all of Ignatius's brothers, with the exception of Pero López, who became a priest and rector of Azpeitia, had entered or were soon to enter the service of the Spanish crown, either bearing arms or taking part in the conquest of the Americas. Ignatius was only five when his brother, Juan Pérez, died in Naples of wounds received in battle. Hernando, another brother, set sail for America in 1510 and died in Panama. Yet another brother, whose name is unknown, died in Hungary fighting the Turks, who were then threatening Vienna.

As the youngest son of the family, Ignatius would almost automatically have been destined for a priestly or clerical career. He would have done his earliest studies with other boys of the parish, or possibly at home with a tutor. It is known that later at Arévalo, as a page to King Ferdinand's treasurer, Juan Velásquez de Cuéllar, Ignatius took pains to improve his already fine handwriting and was appreciated for his excellent penmanship. He learned the traditional dances of the country, such as the *danza real*, popular in Azpeitia, which was accompanied by fifes, tambourines and bagpipes. To the end of his life Ignatius remembered the dances and songs of the Basque country. In his later years, when in low spirits, he would invite a Jesuit priest to his room to play the clavichord, something that delighted him.

Ignatius the Courtier

Arévalo is at the heart of Castile, between Valladolid and Ávila. Dominating the town was the fortress home of Juan Velásquez de Cuéllar. It was the official residence of the *Gran Contador*, the Treasurer of Castile, which was the office held by de Cuéllar. The infante, Don Fernando, who would become the Holy Roman Emperor in 1556, was reared in Juan Velásquez's home.

Ignatius was about sixteen when he went to Arévalo to serve as a page. For nine or ten years, he was brought up with Velásquez's twelve children. The three youngest of the six boys became his constant companions. With them he learned to ride, use his sword and flirt with girls.

Ignatius's days at Arévalo were passed in the afterglow of the renaissance inspired by Queen Isabella of Spain, who had died in 1504. She had initiated a religious, literary and artistic revival in Castile. As well as giving her backing to Christopher Columbus's voyage of discovery, she patronised the University of Salamanca and, with Francisco Jiménez de Cisneros, Archbishop of Toledo, founded the University of Alcalá. Queen Isabella also encouraged the printing of books.

For thirty-six years Queen Isabella's mother had lived in the castle of Arévalo. King Ferdinand (+1516) is known to have stayed there eleven times, occasionally for a whole week. From this fact, we can be almost certain that Ignatius would have seen King Ferdinand and his vast royal entourage, a sight that must have made some impression on the young page. This is the society in which the adolescent Ignatius moved.

The interior walls of the de Cuéllar residence were covered with tapestries depicting scenes from the romance *Amadis of Gaul*.[2] Its chapel was well known for its music. At times, Ignatius would have taken lessons from Juan de Anchieta, a Basque related to him on his mother's side, who was one of the most distinguished Spanish musicians of his day. It was perhaps from Anchieta that Ignatius learnt to play the lute. He was thrilled by the sound of refined court music.

Although Ignatius may have received the clerical tonsure before leaving his home in Loyola, he must have soon made it quite clear that he had no ambition of following a clerical career. In what is sometimes called *The Autobiography*,[3] we read, 'Until the age of twenty-six he was a man given up to the vanities of the world, and his chief delight used to be in the exercise of arms.'[4] Ignatius's later secretary in the Society of Jesus, Juan de Polanco, wrote of the young Ignatius:

> Up to this time [of his conversion], although very much attached to the faith, he did not live in keeping with his belief or guard himself from sins; he was particularly careless about gambling, affairs with women, brawls and the use of arms; this, however, was through force of habit.[5]

Once, on a visit home to Loyola while he was still in the service of Velásquez de Cuellar, Ignatius was involved in a local brawl in which he and his priest-brother, Pero López, attacked the parish clergy. There is a record of the fracas in the correctional court of Guipúzcoa. It seems that Ignatius was the gang leader. The riot took place on carnival day, Shrove Tuesday, 20 February 1515. Ignatius's crimes were said to be 'heinous [*enormes*], premeditated and committed at night'. The judge described Ignatius as 'bold and defiant, cunning, violent and vindictive'. He was armed with sword, dagger, pistol and breastplate, obviously well prepared for the struggle. In any event, Ignatius somehow seems to have been excused his blatant misdemeanours.[6] It is possible that he invoked his clerical status and had recourse to the Church in order to escape a severe penalty.[7]

In the Viceroy's Household

Juan Velásquez de Cuéllar died suddenly on 12 August 1517. A new post was found for Ignatius by Juan Velásquez's widow, María de Velasco, who gave him five hundred coins and two horses to visit Don Antonio Manique de Lara, Duke of Nájera, Viceroy of Navarre. Although he was a skilful swordsman at this stage, contrary to popular belief and legend Ignatius was never a professional soldier. He spent three years as a gentleman of the Viceroy-Duke's household, and during most of that time he remained in Pamplona. Apart from the famous episode of the battle of Pamplona, Ignatius's delight in the vanity of arms was limited to participating in tournaments, duels and challenges of honour.

One of Ignatius's early biographers, the Jesuit Pedro de Ribadeneira, confessed that Ignatius's later mild manner and peaceful gravity were actually cover-ups for a choleric temperament that had been subdued.[8] According to Ribadeneira, Ignatius as a young man was vigorous and polished, and very much enamoured of finery and being well dressed.

Not too long after the outrageous brawl in Loyola, Ignatius seems to have been up to his old tricks again. Francisco de Oya, a dependant of the Countess of Camiña, either in a duel or street fight, actually wounded Ignatius, and made no secret of his intention to kill him. For self-protection, Ignatius petitioned King Charles V of Spain for permission to carry arms and to go about with two bodyguards. This is among the first extant letters of Ignatius.[9] The royal licence was granted on 10 November 1519, but was restricted to one year and to one guard. It would seem that this threat to his life was caused by some rivalry between Ignatius and de Oya over a young lady.

Thus, Ignatius was very much a man of the world, little bothered about the things of God and about sincere personal religious practice. This would soon change.

CHAPTER 2

Injury and Convalescence

By 1521, a French invasion of the kingdom of Navarre in north-eastern Spain was imminent. King Francis I of France wanted to restore Henri d'Albret to his hereditary kingdom of Navarre, but the king's true motive was to bring the war against King Charles V of Spain into Spain itself.[10] After taking the city of Pamplona, Francis planned to advance into Castile. Pamplona was key to the conquest of the province. An army of some 12,000 French infantry and 800 lancers assembled with twenty-nine pieces of artillery. To meet this force, the Duke of Nájera could put into the field of battle only three thousand infantry and seven hundred horse. When the invasion began, two elder brothers of a young Navarese, Francis Xavier, left home to join the French army. This historical enmity between Ignatius and the Xavier family in Pamplona may partly explain Ignatius's early difficulties in winning over Francis Xavier during their years studying together in Paris.

The city of Pamplona fell without a fight. Only the citadel remained to be taken. While his fellow officers were for surrender, Ignatius held out for defence. He was able to persuade the garrison commander to fight on in the hope of holding out until reinforcements arrived. Ignatius judged it disreputable to retreat or surrender. Honour was everything to him. To prepare himself for possible death, in the absence of a priest Ignatius made his confession to a companion soldier, a practice recommended in current manuals of confession of the time.

The bombardment of the citadel continued for six hours. The walls were finally breached. Ignatius was struck by a shot that passed between his legs, shattering the right leg and leaving a gaping flesh wound in the left. The French were victorious, but they were chivalrous in victory. They set Ignatius's right leg and dressed his wounds. He had fallen on 23 or 24 May 1521. Some nine days later, he left Pamplona on a litter and was carried back home to Loyola, probably by his own men.

A Slow Recovery

It was Ignatius's sister-in-law, Magdalena de Aroaz, formerly lady-in-waiting to Queen Isabella, who welcomed the badly wounded fighter home to the Castle of Loyola where he was to lie on his sickbed for nine months, from June 1521 until February 1522. His bedroom was in the upper storey of the Loyola castle. It contained a painting of the Annunciation to the Virgin Mary given to Magdalena as a wedding gift by Queen Isabella. The painting still hangs in what is called the Room of the Conversion in the Castle of Loyola.

Initially, Ignatius's medical condition deteriorated. The physicians and surgeons agreed that his right leg should be broken again and the bones reset. During the operation, Ignatius did not utter a single word and gave no indication that he was in agony, except for a clenching of his fist. He was being the perfect knight, for the clenched fist was the only manifestation of pain permitted by the code of chivalry.

The strain of the operation brought Ignatius close to death. On 24 June, he was advised to make his final confession. On the vigil of the feast of Saints Peter and Paul, 28 June, Ignatius had an extraordinary experience. He thought he saw St Peter assisting him and nursing him back to health. He began to pray fervently to St Peter, to whom he promised to devote his life as a knight should he recover. Within three hours he was judged to be out of danger.

This second operation, however, was not fully successful. As the bones knitted, it was found that a stump had been left protruding from the damaged leg. Ignatius had 'a vain and overweening desire to win renown' in the exercise of arms, and not only would this protuberance be instantly observed, but it would prevent him from wearing the elegant, close-fitting knee boots of the hidalgo.[11] Something had to be done to avoid such a humiliation. In desperation, Ignatius insisted on a third operation. The offending bone would have to be sawn off. While the surgeons did their horrific work, Ignatius was once again silent. In the end, the operation was successful and the disfigurement was hardly noticeable, although Ignatius was left with a slight limp until the end of his days.

Conflicting Attractions

During his recovery, when he felt well enough, Ignatius suffered from extreme boredom, so he asked for some romantic tales of the kind he had already read so avidly. There were none to be had in the castle of Loyola. Instead, he was given a copy of the *Life of Christ* by the Carthusian monk, Ludolph of Saxony (c.1295–1378) which had been translated into Spanish and printed in Alcalà in four volumes in 1502–3. The Christ that Ludolph presents is the summit of the ideals of the medieval knight. Ludolph writes of the pilgrimages to Jerusalem that already formed part of the traditional devotions of the people of Guipùzcoa, and this idea of pilgrimage to Jerusalem would soon become important for Ignatius.

Ignatius was also given the *Lives of the Saints*, consisting of selected biographies of saints by the Italian Dominican, Jacopo de Voragine, Archbishop of Genoa, who died in 1298.[12] The book, known in the original as the *Legenda Aurea* – The Golden Legend – had been translated into Spanish as early as 1480. The saints, especially the founders of religious orders, were presented as *cabelleros de Dios,* knights in the service of the eternal prince, Jesus Christ.

Slowly, certain saints began to appeal to Ignatius. Saints Francis and Dominic were already vaguely familiar to him: a relative on his father's side, Doña Maria de Emparan y Loyola, had founded the convent of Franciscan Tertiaries in Azpeitia and, on his mother's side, a more distant relative, Maria de Guevara, had set up the Poor Clares in the convent of Arévalo, which Juan Velásquez de Cuéllar later endowed.

Another saint who took hold of Ignatius's imagination was St Honofrio or Humphrey, who was either Persian or Ethiopian. A dishevelled solitary from the fourth century, he had become widely popular in Europe thanks to the Crusaders.

As well as reading and pondering on these spiritual books, Ignatius also spent time fantasising about the knightly exploits and amorous trysts he might accomplish as a hidalgo. But he now began to notice the various mood swings that accompanied these times of reflection. It is worth pausing here to quote directly from *The Autobiography*:

> Reading through these [books] often, he was becoming rather attached to what he found written there. But, on ceasing to read them, he would stop to think: sometimes about the things he had read, at other times about the things of the world he had been accustomed to think about before. And, out of the many vain things which had previously presented themselves to him, one held his heart in such deep possession that he was subsequently absorbed in thought about it for two or three and four hours without noticing it, imagining what he would do in the service of a certain lady: the means he would take so as to be able to reach the country where she was, the witty love poems, the words he would say to her, the deeds of arms he would do in her service. He was so carried away by all this that he had no consideration of how impossible it was to be able to attain it. For the lady was not of the ordinary nobility, nor a countess or a duchess, rather her state was higher than any of these. Still Our Lord was helping him, causing some other thoughts, which were born of the things he was reading, to follow these. For while reading the lives of Our Lord and the saints, he would stop to think, reasoning with himself, 'How would it be, if I did this which St Francis did, and this which St Dominic did?' And thus he used to think over many things which he was finding good, always proposing to himself difficult and laborious things. And as he was proposing these, it seemed to him he was finding in himself an ease as regards putting them into practice ...

This succession of such different thoughts lasted a considerable time for him ... Still, there was this difference:

that when he was thinking about the worldly stuff he would take much delight, but when he left it aside after getting tired, he would find himself dry and discontented. But when he thought about going to Jerusalem barefoot ... and about doing all the rigours he was seeing the other saints had done, not only used he be consoled while in such thoughts, but he would remain content and happy even after laying them aside. But he wasn't investigating this, not stopping to ponder this difference, until one time when his eyes were opened a little, and he began to marvel at this difference in kind and to reflect on it, picking up from experience that from some thoughts he would be left sad and from others happy, and little by little coming to know the difference in kind of spirits that were stirring: the one from the devil, and the other from God.[13]

The identity of the lady of Ignatius's reveries has never been established. Several ladies of royal rank whom Ignatius may have known personally have been proposed. It is more than likely that he was dreaming about some royal princess. However, this is of secondary importance. What is of real importance in the quotation above is that this is the first mention of Ignatius's making a distinction between the contrasting moods which would arise in him as a result of his reflecting on the things of God and, for want of a better phrase, on worldly matters. Recognising this distinction will become vitally important in Ignatius's teaching of what he later termed 'the discernment of spirits'.

One night during his recuperation, unable to sleep, Ignatius felt that he saw clearly before him the likeness of Our Lady with the Child Jesus, and he was filled with sheer happiness, which lasted many hours. Notice again his emphasis on the positive feelings that endured. He also became conscious of some mysterious presence that gave him a total revulsion from his previous dissolute life.

A Fresh Start

Now, when the family and household of Loyola came to visit him in his sickroom, they found a different Ignatius from the worldly hidalgo they had previously known. Much to their surprise, Ignatius began to speak to them of the things of God. This was the beginning of what will be a central work or ministry for Ignatius in the future: having spiritual conversations with people. From this time, he began to realise that such conversations 'helped souls', to use his own expression. He also drew comfort from looking out the window of the castle in Loyola and gazing up at the sky and the stars. As soon as he was able to move about the room, Ignatius began noting in a book passages from the New Testament, marking Christ's words in red and Our Lady's in blue; then he would stop and pray. He began to feel in himself 'a great impetus towards serving our Lord'.[14]

Ignatius eventually recovered from his long illness. Martín, witnessing the gradual interior change that had come over his brother, feared that Ignatius would do something foolish and throw away his future prospects. One day, he brought him around the castle of Loyola, pointing out to him all the material possessions that had been amassed there, and begging him to act sensibly and to do nothing rash.

But Ignatius had made up his mind to leave it all behind. To avoid his brother's wrath, he hinted to Martín that he intended to go to Navarette, where the Duke of Nájara lived. Riding on a mule, Ignatius left Loyola in February 1522, accompanied by two servants, Andrés de Marbaitz and Juan de Landeta, who were sent along to make sure that he arrived at his destination. His brother Pedro, the priest, was also part of the group. They stopped off at the wayside chapel of Aránzazu, a favoured Basque shrine to Our Lady. There, Ignatius kept an all-night vigil in front of the small dark statue of the Madonna set on a carved thorn bush. This statue is still to be seen over the high altar in what is now a large basilica and place of pilgrimage.

The next day, Ignatius and Pedro paid a visit to their sister Magdalena in nearby Oñate, accompanied by the two servants. Here, the two brothers bade farewell to one another. They would never see each other again. Still accompanied by the two servants, Ignatius continued on his journey to Navarette, where he intended to collect some money that the Duke of Nájera owed him. We do not know if Ignatius met the duke on that occasion, but he did request the duke's treasurer to give him the money that was his due. Ignatius took the money, asking that part of it be paid to unspecified persons to whom he was still in debt; the rest of it was to be used to refurbish a statue of the Blessed Virgin that was in poor condition.

Ignatius now parted company with the two servants, who could truthfully report to Martín that he had indeed gone to the duke's palace, and set off alone on the road to Saragossa. Along the way, he came across a Muslim riding in the same direction. They got into conversation together. Strangely, perhaps, their talk turned to the subject of Our Lady's virginity. The Moor agreed that Mary had conceived unaided by man, but would not accept at all that she remained a virgin after childbirth. Ignatius and the Moor argued heatedly about this matter. When they parted Ignatius, still the knight, thought that he had allowed the honour of Our Lady to be besmirched, and wondered if he was bound to ride after the Moor and strike him dead with his dagger. Uncertain if such drastic action would be the proper thing to do, Ignatius allowed the mule on which he rode to decide the matter for him. When they came to a fork in the road, Ignatius gave the mule free rein. The mule took a different road from that taken by the Moor, so the poor man was saved from Ignatius's intentions that day! This amusing yet potentially disastrous episode shows how naive Ignatius's outwardly enthusiastic faith was at this early stage.

Montserrat

Along the road, Ignatius stopped off at the great Benedictine monastery of Our Lady of Montserrat. At the time the community of Benedictine monks numbered about fifty. Ignatius reached the monastery on 21 March 1522. It was twelve years since the death of the Montserrat's most famous abbot, Garcia Jiménez de Cisneros (1455–1510), whose name Ignatius would have heard at Arévalo. Cisneros had first reformed the Benedictine monastery in Valladolid and then introduced his reform in Montserrat, where he built the cloister, established a school, set up a printing press and wrote a popular book entitled *Exercitatorio de la Vida Espiritual*, a manual of the spiritual life printed on the premises in 1500. This book was given to Ignatius by one of the monks, a Frenchman, Jean Chanon, to whom Ignatius made his general confession. This confession, according to Ignatius himself, took him three full days. The monastery of Montserrat still exists to this day, magnificently situated high above the valley and surrounded by dramatic mountain peaks. With its thriving Benedictine community and world-renowned choir school, it is a very popular pilgrimage spot to this day.

On the evening of his third day at the monastery, Ignatius sought out a beggar, gave him the fine clothes he was wearing and put on the loose sackcloth of a pilgrim. He then went to kneel before the statute of the Black Madonna of Montserrat, where spent the whole night in prayer. He hung up his sword and dagger at the shrine, gave his mule to the monastery and left. It was 25 March 1522, and he was thirty-one years old.

CHAPTER 3

Manresa

I gnatius's first destination was the town of Manresa, below Montserrat, where he initially intended to stay for only a few days. In fact, he ended up staying for about ten months. Manresa was a small industrial town of a few thousand inhabitants. It was then famous for its cotton manufacturing. It was on the way down from the monastery of Montserrat to Manresa that Ignatius first met Iñes Pascual. She owned a shop and thriving business in the centre of Barcelona and would later be a very generous benefactress to him.

Early Days

On his arrival in Manresa on 25 March 1522, Ignatius asked to be taken in at the hospice of Santa Lucía where, in return for a roof – in fact, a dark and narrow cell – he would help to look after the house. He attended daily Mass at either the cathedral or the Dominican friary, during which he would read an account of the Passion of Our Lord. In the evenings, he attended sung vespers and compline in the large Gothic basilica. He confessed and went to communion weekly, an unusual practice in those days when people received these sacraments much less frequently; indeed, such regular reception of the Eucharist was discouraged. Ignatius, in contrast, encouraged some women of Manresa to confess and take communion every Sunday, to do good works and to serve the Lord.[15] In imitation of the saints, he himself visited the sick in the hospitals where he would bathe the infirm. The children of Manresa would sometimes follow him shouting 'the holy man' or 'the sackcloth man' – a reference to his pilgrim attire. In passing, it is important to note here that in *The Autobiography* Ignatius always refers to himself as 'the pilgrim'. This is how he saw himself, as someone following in the footsteps of his new-found Lord, travelling along the path of discipleship. During Ignatius's canonisation processes (1582–1606), many witnesses from Manresa came forward to testify that he had arrived in Manresa dressed in sackcloth. They called him 'the holy man' because of his penance, continual prayers and fasting.

During his first four months at Manresa, as Ignatius recounted afterwards, he was in a constant state of happiness, but without knowing a thing about the inner working of the spirit. 'Up to this time he had always persisted almost in one identical interior state, with largely unvarying happiness.'[16] Ignatius started recording his spiritual experiences in a notebook, making notes that would later form the basis of his classic work, *The Spiritual Exercises*.

Darkness and Light

Suddenly Ignatius's mood changed. He began to be tortured by scruples, wondering whether he had confessed properly at the monastery of Montserrat. No one he consulted could rid him of his doubts. Although he kept to seven hours' prayer during the day, his torments went on for several months. He was even afflicted with the thought of suicide. He passed a whole week without food, breaking his fast only on the order of his confessor. Relief came with a sudden illumination or inspiration, bringing with it a resolve never again to confess his past sins or to allow himself to be troubled by scruples.

Ignatius then began to experience a deep serenity and peace that never left him for the rest of his life. He attached great importance to feelings, especially feelings of deep, inner peace that were not fleeting but lasting. Could it be that such feelings of peace and calm were indications of God's will in his life, what he would call 'the good spirit'? Could it be that their opposite, feelings of inner turmoil, distaste, confusion, uncertainty, were indications of what he would term 'the evil spirit'?

In his spiritual life, Ignatius began to understand that God was treating him 'in the same way as a schoolmaster deals with a child, teaching him'.[17] He wasn't sure if this was because of his own stupidity or because he had no one to teach him. The saints began to recede into the background, and their place in Ignatius's thoughts and prayers was taken up more and more by Jesus and the Blessed Trinity.

The Autobiography states that 'one day while saying the Office of Our Lady on the steps of the monastery, his understanding began to be elevated so that he saw the Most Holy Trinity in the form of three musical keys. This brought on so many tears and so much sobbing that he could not control himself.' Other matters were 'revealed to his understanding' as well in those days, concerning the creation of the world, the Eucharistic presence and the person of Christ. So powerful were these experiences that he believed that 'even if there were no scriptures to teach these matters of faith, he would be resolved to die for them, only because of what he had seen'.[18]

One day Ignatius sat in prayer above the River Cardoner. Suddenly, 'his understanding was opened and though he saw no vision he perceived and understood many things both spiritual and touching matters of faith and learning.'[19] He admitted later that he could not put into words what he had been given to understand at that time. It was a total mystical view of the world that he had been given. He saw how all things proceeded from God and returned to their Trinitarian origin, and how all the mysteries of the Christian faith were interlocked in that movement. Ignatius said afterwards that whatever he had learned at other times, either by study or personal effort or supernatural light, was less than he had received at that moment.

Diego Laínez, one of Ignatius' early companions in the Society of Jesus and his eventual successor as superior general, later said that 'in one hour Ignatius learned more from God than he could ever have been taught by all the doctors of the world'.[20] A second-generation Jesuit, Jerónimo Nadal, who was one of Ignatius's right-hand men in the early Society, said of Ignatius, 'In almost all his decisions [he] customarily cited the outstanding illumination, even when he governed the Society in Rome,' and he did so as though in Manresa 'he had seen the reasons for or causes of everything'.[21]

Ignatius himself never ventured to speak categorically about his mystical experiences, but always prefaced his remarks with phrases like 'It seemed to him' or 'It appeared that'. Intriguingly, Laínez says that Ignatius, despite his limited education, began to write a book on the Trinity at this stage, and his later biographer, Pedro de Ribadeneira, adds that this attempt had reached some eighty pages.[22] Unfortunately, no trace of this work has ever been found

It seems that Ignatius lived for much of his time in Manresa in the hospice of Santa Lucía, but he also availed of other accommodation from time to time. After an initial spell in the hospice, he was given a cell on the ground floor of the Dominican priory of St Peter in April 1522. He seems to have stayed there for only twelve or thirteen days at that stage, returning again the following August when he was struggling with scruples. In the meantime, he spent some time in accommodation offered by the Amigant family, who lived in the main square of Manresa. Ignatius did not, as is often said, live in a cave during his stay in Manresa, and in fact he makes no mention of a cave himself. Yet so many early witnesses recall the 'holy cave' that their testimonies deserve to be taken into account. There is a hill with a cave on the outskirts of Manresa, and it appears that Ignatius regularly went to this cave to pray, almost certainly remaining there all night on some occasions. The Church of the Holy Cave was built in 1767, but services were a not held there until 1867. The modern would-be pilgrim will be happy to hear that heating was installed in 1990!

During these ten months in Manresa, Ignatius had learned to read or discern his interior moods and movements, to recognise which feelings brought him life, and which feelings had the opposite effect. This is the source of the Ignatian practice of the Examen (see Chapter 23). We would all do well to pause at the end of each day, as prompted by Ignatius, and ask ourselves two simple questions, 'What gave me life today?' and 'What drained me of life?' For Ignatius, the answers to these deceptively simple questions would tell him what he believed to be God's will for him each day. These answers helped Ignatius – and today help those who follow Ignatian spirituality – to 'find God in all things'.

Sharing his Vision

As previously mentioned, it was from this period at Manresa that Ignatius formed many of the ideas upon which he based what was later to become his spiritual classic, the *Spiritual Exercises*. This little book was the fruit of his personal experience of prolonged prayer and illuminations, both at Loyola and, especially, at Manresa. Although he later altered, augmented and perfected what he wrote at the time, the outline of the *Spiritual Exercises* was there before he left Manresa for Jerusalem.

The Spiritual Exercises is an unusual book. Even in its final version, from 1541, it was rough and rudimentary in form. Rather than a book to be read, it is a guide for the one who gives the Exercises to another, to be translated into concrete practice according to circumstances. Juan de Polanco, Ignatius's later secretary in the Society of Jesus, wrote, 'Thus it was in Manresa that he began to give the Exercises to various persons and in this way the Lord visited them with revelations and consolations, blessing them with an admirable taste for spiritual things and an increase of all virtues.'[23]

During the final months of 1522, and until his departure for Jerusalem, Ignatius felt eager to help other people who came looking for him to discuss their interior lives. He would sometimes give spiritual talks in the little chapel of Santa Lucía to the devout women of Manresa.

CHAPTER 4

Pilgrimage to Jerusalem

A s Ignatius lay recuperating on his sickbed at Loyola, he had resolved to go on pilgrimage to Jerusalem, where he could walk the roads and streets that Jesus had walked. Now, finally, that goal was in view. Ignatius left Manresa around the middle of February 1523; he had to be in Rome at Easter to obtain the pope's permission for his pilgrimage to Jerusalem. This was the ruling of Pope Clement V (1305–20) given at the Council of Vienne (1311–12) for all intending pilgrims to Jerusalem.

The Journey to Venice
Ignatius walked from Manresa to Barcelona. In Barcelona, he met up again with Iñes Pascual, the lady whom he had earlier met on the road from Montserrat to Manresa. Iñes gave him a room in her house near the harbour where he waited for two or three weeks for a boat sailing to Italy. In Barcelona, Ignatius met another lady who was to feature prominently in his life, Isabel Roser, the wife of Juan Roser, a wealthy businessman. Quite by chance, Isabel spotted Ignatius sitting down with some children on the altar steps of a local church. Later, she would tell the young Jesuit, Pedro de Ribadeneira, that she saw Ignatius's head 'gleaming on all sides and emitting something like very bright rays'.[24] Isabel became one of Ignatius's most generous benefactors and would feature prominently in the early history of the Society of Jesus.

Ignatius was determined to put himself unreservedly in the hands of divine providence. Before boarding the boat that would take him to Italy, he left five or six small coins on a bench on the waterfront. The boat made the crossing to Gaeta in five days. On disembarking, Ignatius set out to walk the 120 kilometres to Rome. He reached the city on Palm Sunday, 19 March 1523. He spent Holy Week in Rome in prayer and begging alms. Just two days after his arrival, he received permission from the office of Pope Adrian VI (1522–23) to visit the Holy Land. The papal document giving him permission is preserved to this day in the Vatican archives, and is made out to 'Iñigo de Loyola, cleric of the diocese of Pamplona'.

Ignatius then left Rome to walk to Venice, a journey of about 600 kilometres. He lived by begging along the way and, on reaching Venice, slept in St Mark's Square. Eventually, he accepted the hospitality of a Spaniard, most likely one of the *tolmazzi* appointed annually to care for pilgrims and provide them with lodgings and other necessities for the voyage. This Spaniard even introduced Ignatius to the Doge of Venice, Andrea Gritti, who gave instructions that Ignatius should be given free passage on a state vessel taking the new Venetian governor to Cyprus.

The Holy Land

Ignatius and his fellow passengers set sail on the *Negrona* and reached Cyprus on 14 August 1523, exactly a calendar month after leaving Venice. The pilgrims then journeyed on to Jaffa, arriving there on 31 August. They arrived in Jerusalem five days later, on 4 September. The following day, under the guidance of the Franciscans who had charge of Christian pilgrims, Ignatius did the round of the holy sites in the city.

All, however, did not go according to Ignatius's plans. His initial intention had been to stay in Jerusalem in order to convert the Muslims, dying there for Christ if necessary. But tensions were high in that part of the world, as they often have been, and pilgrims to the holy sites were in danger of abduction or worse. The obligation of ransoming captured pilgrims fell on the Franciscans, who now ordered all Christian pilgrims to leave Jerusalem at once for their own safety. Ignatius, however, was adamant that he would stay. He would renounce his own plans only if he could be shown that he would be sinning by remaining in Jerusalem. It was then that the Franciscan Provincial, Fr Marco de Salodio, said that he possessed papal bulls giving him the power to expel pilgrims or allow them to stay – and also the power to excommunicate those who did not obey him. This was enough for Ignatius. He would leave without further question or protest. However, before he left Jerusalem, under cover of darkness, he slipped out one last time to the Mount of Olives. He wanted to see, from the supposed imprints of Jesus' feet on a stone, which way Jesus was facing at his ascension. For some reason, he wanted to imprint this image on his memory.

CHAPTER 5

Studies in Barcelona

On 23 September 1523, Ignatius left Jerusalem. He arrived in Venice in mid-January 1524 and stayed there until mid-February. It was probably in late February or early March that he arrived back in Barcelona. Although he was already in his thirty-fourth year, Ignatius now resolved to study so that he might be better prepared to 'help souls'. Some ladies of Barcelona befriended him, attracted by his obvious goodness and sincerity in his pursuit of God, and they became his main support during his long years of study, not only in Barcelona but also in Alcalá, Salamanca and Paris.

Studying Latin

Barcelona had no university, but its schools formed a kind of consortium where the classical Latin authors were taught. Thanks to his friends, Ignatius was accepted without charge as a pupil of Jerónimo Ardévol, a strict, able and inspiring teacher in the school of grammar. Ignatius, however, encountered a problem. When he tried to memorise Latin declensions and conjugations, he was wildly distracted by powerful new insights into spiritual things. Deciding that it was a subtle temptation of the evil spirit 'under the appearance of an angel of light' that was keeping him from his studies, he talked frankly to his teacher, promising henceforth to apply himself without distraction to his work and not to miss any of his classes.[25]

Ignatius lodged at Iñes Pascual's house close to the Church of Santa

Maria del Mar where he worshipped and where he met his teacher to discuss his difficulties. He did not eat with the Pascual family but, after begging his food from door to door, sorted out on his return all he had been given, setting out three portions, one for the poor, one for the sick and the final one for himself. His room was an attic measuring fifteen feet by thirteen feet. It was no more than five feet high. Ignatius slept on the floor.

Also living in Barcelona was Isabel Roser, who belonged to the Catalan nobility. Her marriage had been childless. In social and academic circles, the family was very influential in Barcelona and it was probably to them that Ignatius owed his introduction to Ardévol.

At the convent of Santa Clara in Barcelona, founded in 1233 for Poor Clares but now following the Benedictine Rule, Ignatius may have met the saintly nun Teresa Rejadella for the first time. Teresa was to become the leader of a group of eleven sisters anxious for reform. Over the years, she became the recipient of some of Ignatius's finest letters of spiritual direction. His initial attempt to bring back the nuns in the convent to a regular life ended in a severe beating by young gallants who frequented the place to satisfy their lust. One can understand why Sister Teresa was hoping for reform.

Early Companions

Ignatius's secretary in later years, Juan de Polanco, alluded to these Barcelona years when he said, 'Ignatius began from that time on to have a desire to gather certain persons to himself in order to put into operation the plan he had, beginning at that time, of helping repair the defects he saw in serving God, namely, persons who might be like trumpets of Jesus Christ.'[26] His first companions were Calixto de Sa, Juan de Arteaga and Lope de Cáceres. They followed Ignatius when he left Barcelona, but their initial enthusiasm dimmed with time and they eventually went their separate ways.

At the end of his second year of Latin studies, Ardévol told Ignatius that he was now competent enough to begin his course in arts and philosophy, and recommended that he go to the University of Alcalà, thirty-five kilometers north-east of Madrid. So, in early spring of 1526, Ignatius set out on foot for Alcalà, a journey of some 600 kilometres.

CHAPTER 6
Alcalà and Salamanca

I gnatius arrived in Alcalà in March 1526, followed by Calixto de San, Juan de Arteaga and Lope de Cáceres. Alcalà was at that time the focus of the humanist movement in Spain.[27] The university of Alcalà had been founded in 1510 by Cardinal Francisco Ximenez de Cisneros (1436–1517), the friar archbishop of Toledo. It was thanks to Cisneros that the celebrated polyglot bible – in Latin, Greek, Hebrew and Chaldaic – was produced with the aid of Jewish scholars and published in 1522, four years after Cisneros's death.

Suspicions of the Inquisition
On reaching Alcalà, Ignatius took up residence in the hospice of Antezana. He registered his name on the roster of poor students. In addition to his studies, Ignatius soon began holding spiritual meetings in the hospice and in the homes of those who invited him to a meal. He was also busy giving spiritual direction to those who sought his help and teaching Christian doctrine to those who gathered around him. He wore a type of clerical garb, with a plain grey hood for protection against the sun and rain. All the while he kept up his mendicant way of life, begging on behalf of himself and others. At that time, Ignatius and his three companions dressed themselves in the same type of poor cloth. The material they wore led people to call them *ensayalados*, meaning 'those dressed in sackcloth'.

A year before Ignatius's arrival in Alcalà, the Spanish Inquisition had moved with force against a group called the *alumbrados*, which was attracting followers at the time.[28] They had meeting houses where they would read and comment on passages of the Bible, and where prayer gatherings were conducted. They preferred mental prayer to vocal prayer. They distanced themselves, at least psychologically, from ordinary Christians. They claimed to be moved by intense mystical communication on the part of the Holy Spirit. They repudiated the mediation of the Church, especially the hierarchy and the sacraments, while seeking direct communication with God.

During their time in Alcalà, Ignatius and his companions were sometimes known as *Iniguistas*, and in the mind of some people they became associated with the *alumbrados*. Then rumours and false reports began to circulate about Ignatius and his meetings with certain ladies. The Archbishop of Toledo's representative, Juan Rodríguez de Figueroa, heard reports of strange swoonings and convulsions that were taking place among the women associates of Ignatius. He was summoned before the Inquisition to explain his teaching, but nothing reprehensible was found in either his conduct or his teaching.[29] He insisted that he did not preach but merely talked in a familiar way about the things of God. Since Ignatius's followers were not members of a religious order, Figueroa cautioned them not to dress in a way that suggested that they were. He also forbade Ignatius to go around with bare feet. Being fully compliant with any such orders given by a legitimate Church authority, Ignatius immediately put on shoes.

For four months, Ignatius was left undisturbed. However, on 16 March 1527 a new investigation was opened. This time it was more rigorous. It concerned the lessons that Ignatius was giving; he called them 'spiritual exercises'. While awaiting examination by the Inquisition, he was put in prison. The sentence given on 1 June 1527 obliged Ignatius and his friend, Calixto, to get rid of their eccentric habits and wear instead the dress of ordinary students. It seems that Figueroa had been impressed by Ignatius's respectful conduct under examination, however, since he bought him all he needed, including his clothes, cap and academic gear.

Only one line in Ignatius's autobiography refers to his studies in Alcalà: 'There he studied the Logic of Soto, the Physics of Albert and Peter Lombard.'[30] He had, in fact, made very little progress in his studies in Alcalà. His days were mainly spent explaining Christian doctrine, holding conversations on spiritual matters and gathering food for himself and the poor.

Among the people whom Ignatius befriended while in Alcalà was Martín de Olave, a Basque student. He gave Ignatius alms on his arrival and would later join the Society of Jesus. He subsequently obtained a doctorate in theology at the University of Paris, and became a brilliant professor at the Roman College. Another acquaintance of Ignatius in Alcalà was Manuel Miona, a Portuguese priest who was then Ignatius's confessor. It was Miona who introduced Ignatius to the *Enchiridion* of Desiderius Erasmus. Miona would also become a Jesuit. Interestingly, the printer of the first Spanish translation of the *Enchiridion*, a priest called Diego de Eguia, joined the Society at a later date. We are told by Luís Gonçalves da Câmara that Ignatius, in later life, declined to read the *Enchiridion* because he felt that Erasmus was dampening his spiritual fervour.[31] Da Câmara adds that Ignatius steered clear of Erasmus because preachers and men of authority criticised him, and because he, Ignatius, preferred reading books 'upon which there was no shadow of doubt', such as *The Imitation of Christ*, which he had first read in Manresa.[32]

Further Reversals

In late June, Ignatius and his companions left Alcalà. Ignatius sought out the Archbishop of Toledo, Alonzo de Fonseca, primate of Spain, who was in Valladolid in attendance at the royal court.[33] Surprisingly, perhaps, Ignatius had no difficulty in getting an audience, and the archbishop was clearly impressed with him. He told Ignatius that he had friends in Salamanca where he had founded a college for poor students, and that Ignatius should go and study there. So Ignatius set out, walking as ever, on the 120-kilometre journey to Salamanca.

In the fourteenth century, the university of Salamanca had been among the leading four or five universities in Europe, with an enrolment of about 14,000 students. Following the establishment of the University of Alcalà, however, its numbers had declined.

Shortly after his arrival in Salamanca, around 20 June 1527, Ignatius and his companion Calixto were invited to dine with the Dominicans.[34] Asked by his hosts what matters he was preaching, Ignatius said that he only spoke about the things of God. The Dominican sub-prior, Nicolás de Santo Tomás, was suspicious, however, and Ignatius and Calixto were held for three days in the priory. After this, a notary of the Inquisition marched them off to prison.

Martín Frías, Vicar-General of the Archbishop of Salamanca, took Ignatius's precious notes of the *Spiritual Exercises* away to be examined. This is the first time that Ignatius alludes to the *Spiritual Exercises* specifically in *The Autobiography*.[35] Ignatius was summoned before four judges; three were doctors of law, and the fourth was Frías himself. All four judges had read the *Spiritual Exercises*. After three weeks and a day in prison, Ignatius and Calixto were released and told that they and their companions could go on teaching, provided they did not attempt to define what constituted grave sin until they had completed another four years of study. Less than twenty days after his release, Ignatius set out on the road to Barcelona on the first stage of his journey to Paris. Given all of the interference from the Inquisition in Salamanca, he had resolved to continue his studies at the University of Paris. He left behind his companions, who were to join him later when he had raised enough money for their support. As it turned out, none of them followed him to Paris.

In Barcelona, Ignatius stayed in the Pascual house for three months. In December he set out for Paris – on foot, as usual – a journey of more than 1,000 kilometres.

CHAPTER 7

Paris

In the time of Ignatius, the University of Paris consisted of some thirty colleges. Ignatius registered at the Collège de Montaigu in February 1528. The Montaigu was located on what is now known as the rue Laplace, near the Panthéon. This college was popular with Spaniards and Portuguese, and ran courses in Latin grammar, composition and literature. It also catered for teenage boys. Ignatius, by contrast, was thirty-seven years old at this stage!

Penniless in Paris
One of Ignatius's later companions, Diego Laínez, said that Ignatius studied without aiming for honours or high positions, or any human reward at all. His studies offered him no enticement to pleasure. In fact, he shrank from study, because of his own natural disposition and because of his mature age, which was less suited to formal academic work.[36]

The Collège de Montaigu may have been popular with some students, but certainly not with all. Its regime and discipline were very severe. The classes began at five o'clock in the morning and ended in the evening at seven. Two former students of the Montaigu, the Frenchman Rabelais and the Dutchman Erasmus, had horrendous memories of the place. Rabelais branded the college 'a squalid hole where the students lived on rotten eggs, and if they chanced not to die, they emerged as fools or invalids for life'. Erasmus, in one of his *Colloquia*, speaks of leaving the college with 'nothing except an infected body and a vast array of lice'.[37] The reformer John Calvin left the Montaigu about the time Ignatius arrived.[38]

When Ignatius first arrived in Paris, he had received the gift of a sum of money from some Spanish benefactors. He gave the money to a fellow boarder in the hope that this student would keep it safely for him. Instead, the student spent the money on himself and was not able to pay it back later. Ignatius was so needy that he was forced to stay in the hospice of Saint-Jacques-aux-Espagnols in the rue Saint-Denis. The hospice had been founded for pilgrims who were on their way to Santiago de Compostela in Spain. For the first eighteen months of his stay in Paris, until September 1529, Ignatius remained an external student or *martinet* at the Collège de Montaigu.

In Lent 1529, Ignatius interrupted his studies at the Montaigu to make his first begging visit to Flanders. He had been advised to go there by a member of a religious order. During the two months he spent there, he went around begging for his expenses from the well-to-do Spanish merchants in the region. In Bruges, he may have lodged with a Gonzalo de Aguilera and his wife. Gonzalo was a Castilian merchant living in the rue Espagnole, near other compatriots.

With the money received from Flanders and further assistance from his friends in Barcelona, Ignatius moved into quarters of his own in Paris. This made it possible for him to give the Spiritual Exercises during May and June to three Spanish students resident in the university – a Basque, Amador de Elduayen, Pedro de Peralta, already a master of arts, and Juan Castro from Burgos, who was teaching at the Sorbonne University. Having made the Spiritual Exercises, they all made fundamental changes in their lives: they gave their possessions, including their books, to the poor, took to begging in the streets, and left their colleges to live in the hospice of St Jacques.

None of the three remained permanently with Ignatius, however. Castro entered the Carthusian Order in Spain and Peraltra made a pilgrimage to the Holy Land and later became a canon of Toledo. Amador does not reappear in Ignatius's story.

On 1 October 1529, Ignatius moved to the Collège Sainte-Barbe, across from the Montaigu, to begin his three-and-a-half-year course in arts and philosophy. During the vacation of 1530, he made his second begging visit to Flanders, from where he travelled to England in 1531. He writes of this visit, 'Once he even crossed to England and returned with more alms than he usually did in other years.'[39] He doubtless looked for both lodging and funds from the Spanish community living close to the Thames on Old Broad Street in London.

Controversy and Companions

Even though Ignatius was engaged in his studies, he so inspired some outstanding young men in the university that they resolved to renounce their material wealth.[40] Some Spanish noblemen who were connected by bonds of friendship with these new disciples took their decision very badly. Ignatius was considered to be the instigator of these troubles, and so he fell into disfavour with many influential people. Among them was the renowned scholar Pedro Ortiz, who had Ignatius's teaching examined. An accusation against Ignatius was lodged with the Inquisitor, Dominican Matthieu Ory. Ory quickly assured Ignatius that there was no substance in the allegation and that he need not fear.

Having learned from his problems in Alcalà and Salamanca, Ignatius was now determined to make a success of his studies. On one occasion, he promised his teacher, Master Juan de Peña, a Spaniard who was teaching philosophy at Sainte-Barbe, that he would never miss a lecture as long as he had no need to go begging. He also decided to refrain from giving the Spiritual Exercises and similar activities during term time, so that he would not be distracted by other people's affairs and lose sight of his need to study.[41]

Two very different students, in personality at least, shared quarters with Ignatius at Sainte-Barbe. They were Pierre Favre and Francis Xavier. They had a room in a high tower that everyone referred to as 'The Paradise'. Pierre Favre, a young man of fine intellect, was of peasant stock from Savoy in south-eastern France. He was tortured by scruples and was reluctant to receive holy orders. For two years Ignatius, who formed a special bond with him, nursed him through these difficulties. Ignatius, for his part, profited greatly from Favre's helping him in his philosophy studies.[42] To his dying day, Pierre Favre never ceased to thank God for so arranging things that he should teach Ignatius about Aristotle while Ignatius taught him about God:

> May it please the divine clemency to give me the grace of clearly remembering and pondering the benefits which the Lord conferred on me in those days through that man. First-ly, he gave me an understanding of my conscience and of the temptations and scruples I had for so long without either understanding them or seeing the way by which I would be able to get peace.[43]

Francis Xavier was the youngest son of a noble Navarese family, im-poverished after King Ferdinand annexed the province in 1515. When he was twelve years old, he watched the towers of the family castle being torn down. As the youngest in the family, Xavier chose a ca-reer in the Church for himself, but from no lofty motives, for he had the promise of a good benefice. By nature, Xavier was ambitious and full of charm, and a good sportsman. Initially, he despised Ignatius for his impoverished way of living. On 15 March 1530 Xavier received his licentiate in philosophy, and in the following year began teaching. His contract was for three-and-half years, during which time he was to study theology. Ignatius knew Xavier's worth, however. When lectur-ers were competing for students, Ignatius broadcast Xavier's abilities, attended his lectures and increased his reputation. Ignatius famously said of Xavier, 'He was the hardest dough I ever kneaded.' In the end, Xavier succumbed to his spiritual influence.

Others too became Ignatius's friends: Simão Rodriguez, from Por-tugal, and three Spaniards, Diego Laínez, Alfonso Salmerón and Nicolás Bobadilla. Twenty-one-year-old Laínez and eighteen-year-old Salmerón had both been studying in Alcalà, where they had heard about Ignatius. Providentially, Ignatius was the first person Laínez encoun-tered when he arrived at Sainte-Barbe. Bobadilla already had degrees from Alcalà and Valladolid when he arrived in Paris. Rodrigues had one of the scholarships given by King John III of Portugal to support Portuguese students. He had been living at Sainte-Barbe since 1527, but had no direct dealings with Ignatius until 1533. As an old man in

1577, Rodrigues recalled that it was he himself who took the initiative, attracted as he was by the sanctity of this older student who was already in his forties.

Ignatius's only aim at this stage was to inspire these men with his own ideals. Several other students, whose names are not known, were also influenced by him, resolving to confess and communicate regularly. Others entered religious life and persevered in their vocation, some with the Franciscans, some with the Dominicans and others with the Carthusians.

Ignatius received his bachelor's degree in January 1532 and, a little more than a year later, on 13 March 1533, gained a licentiate in philosophy. He was marked thirtieth in a class of one hundred students.[44]

It may seem very naïve to us today, but all of these early companions of Ignatius had resolved to go to Jerusalem on completion of their studies and work there for the conversion of the Muslims as well as in the service of Christians. They also had deep desire to walk the roads where Jesus himself had walked. Ignatius, Laínez and Favre sometimes fantasised about living the rest of their lives in Palestine, giving themselves totally to the service of the Christians and the conversion of the Muslims, whom they referred to as 'infidels'.

Ignatius gave the full Spiritual Exercisesto Pierre Favre in 1534.[45] Favre was ordained priest and said his first Mass on 22 July 1534. Around this time, after much discussion among themselves, these early companions decided to lead a life of poverty in imitation of Jesus in the gospels. Both this decision and their resolve to go to Jerusalem were promises relating to the future, effective from the day they would complete their studies.

On the Feast of the Assumption, 15 August 1534, all seven companions went to the chapel of St Denis in Montmartre, then on the outskirts of Paris, where they pronounced their vows at a Mass celebrated by Pierre Favre. They bound themselves 'to renounce all things (apart from travel provisions), to care for the spiritual welfare of their neighbours and to sail for Jerusalem'.[46] They made one important proviso, however: if their projected pilgrimage to Jerusalem proved impossible, they would offer themselves to the pope in Rome for him to send them where he thought best.

In the next two years they renewed their vows on the Feast of the Assumption. Ignatius was absent from both meetings, but in his absence three more companions had joined the group: Claude Jay, a schoolfellow of Pierre Favre's from Savoy and already a priest, and two other Frenchmen, Jean Codure and Paschase Broët, who had been ordained in 1524.

In the autumn of 1534, Ignatius's health worsened. His previous excessive penances at Manresa had done permanent damage to his health. Nevertheless, he struggled on and received his master's degree on 14 March 1535. In accordance with the thinking of the time, his physicians advised him to return to his native air of Azpeitia. Before that could happen, however, he was again reported to the Inquisition, charged with giving spiritual exercises and receiving communion along with his companions every week at a Carthusian monastery. Receiving communion with such frequency was considered to be presumptuous. This time Ignatius sought out the Inquisitor himself, who assured him again that he had no cause for concern.

While in Paris, Ignatius was constantly revising the notebook that contained his Spiritual Exercises. It was at this time that he added the important meditations on the Two Standards, the Three Kinds of Humility and a number of other important sections.

Ignatius had taken note of his physicians' advice that his health would greatly benefit from exposure to his native air. So, in early April 1535, he bade farewell to his companions. They were to continue with their studies in Paris until January 1537. Then, in the spring of 1537, they were to meet up with Ignatius in Venice, when together they would fulfill their vow of going to the Holy Land. Poor as these companions were, they presented Ignatius with a donkey for the journey home because of his extreme frailty.

CHAPTER 8

Spain and Venice

Ignatius had been away from his home for thirteen years. When he arrived in Loyola, he refused to live at the family castle of his brother Martín Garcia. Instead, he lodged at the hospice of Santa Magdalena, a short distance out of town. He begged alms from door to door, much to his noble brother's shame and annoyance. After all, the family honour was at stake!

Reforms in Loyola

Notwithstanding his brother's annoyance, Ignatius began teaching the children and adults of Loyola the rudiments of the Christian faith. Martín tried to dissuade him by telling him that no one would come to listen to him. Ignatius responded that one would be enough. In fact, many people came to hear Ignatius teach and preach, including, eventually, Martín himself.

Soon Ignatius's talks became daily events. On Sundays and feast days he spoke in the local church. The numbers coming to hear him increased steadily, until eventually they were so numerous that he was forced to address the people in the fields, with some of his listeners climbing the trees to get a better view.[47]

In nearby Azpeitia, as later in Rome, Ignatius was concerned to reduce the scourge of prostitution among the local poor women. He also reconciled a number of local feuding families, and arranged for the

Angelus to be rung three times a day, at morning, noon and evening. He brought about a reform in the behaviour of the local clergy, and saw to it that strict laws were passed to control gambling.

Ignatius did not spend all of his time in Loyola, doubtless to the relief of some! During his stay, he took the opportunity to visit Francis Xavier's home in Navarre, some 170 kilometres away, where Francis's eldest brother, Miguel, lived in the restored Xavier castle. He also visited Alfonso Salmerón's family in Toledo, a journey of some 500 kilometres from Loyola.

Reunion in Venice

Having fulfilled his obligations in Spain, and having regained some physical strength, Ignatius embarked from Valencia for Italy, where he travelled through Genoa and Bologna, eventually reaching Venice. As he awaited the arrival of his companions from Paris, Ignatius resumed his favourite occupation of 'helping souls', giving the Spiritual Exercises to some nobles and people of high rank in the city, among others.

During this time, he also made the acquaintance of Giam Pietro Carafa, who would later become Pope Paul IV.[48] Having resigned from the archbishopric of Chiete in southern Italy, Carafa, along with some others, had formed a religious order of clerics known as the Theatines. Carafa's good intentions for the new religious order were, in Ignatius's view, undermined both by his own extravagant way of life and by the self-interest of its members. Ignatius expressed some of these criticisms frankly in a letter addressed to Carafa, who reacted angrily at the time and retained the bitter memory for years to come.

In early January 1537, the nine companions eventually arrived in Venice from Paris. Favre, Rodrigues, Salmeron, Bobadilla, Jay, Codure and Broët had all recently received their master's degrees, while Laínez and Xavier had obtained theirs earlier. One can only imagine the rejoicing at their coming together again. Ignatius had three new recruits by his side to greet them – Diego de Hocesand the two Eguia brothers, Diego and Miguel, whom Ignatius had first met in Alcalà.[49]

Very soon Ignatius set his companions to work. He divided them into two groups to work in two Venetian hospitals, the Incurables and

Giovanni e Paola. He wanted them to put their theological studies aside for a while and engage in menial chores, making beds, cleaning sores, digging graves and burying the dead. Humble work of this kind would later be required of all Jesuit novices in the first two years of their formation. The whole group of companions still nurtured the dream of going to Jerusalem to aid the Christians and to convert the 'infidels'. In mid-Lent, the companions headed for Rome to seek the pope's permission for the journey, just as Ignatius had done many years previously. For some reason, Ignatius deliberately stayed behind in Venice.

On their eventual arrival in Rome, the companions must have been disconcerted to meet an old acquaintance from their Paris days, Dr Pedro Ortiz. As we have seen, Ortiz at that time was less than happy with Ignatius's influence on some of the brighter young students, and had reported him to the Inquisitor. Now in Rome, Ortiz was the ambassador of the Emperor Charles V to the Holy See. Against all expectations, he embraced the companions with supreme kindness, and escorted them personally to meet with Pope Paul III.

Paul III was an intelligent and astute individual. He was intrigued to find these highly educated young theology students before him and, on the very day of their audience with him, he invited the companions to hold a disputation in his presence on a particular theological question. Paul was obviously impressed, since he not only gave his blessing for their journey to Jerusalem, but personally contributed about sixty gold coins to help them on their way. He also gave the priests among them special permission to absolve certain reserved sins.[50] Those who were not yet priests were given permission to be ordained by any bishop. The companions could not have hoped for a better outcome to their Roman visit.

Back in Venice, on 24 June 1537, the feast of St John the Baptist, Ignatius and those of his companions who were not yet priests were ordained by Vincenzo Negusanti, Bishop of Arbe, in his private chapel. There was one exception, however: Alfonso Salmerón, because of his young age, was ordained a deacon and had to wait another year for priesthood. Shortly before the ceremony, all the companions took vows of poverty and chastity at the hands of the papal nuncio to Venice,

Cardinal Veralli, who now granted them wide-ranging permissions for priestly work in the territories of the Venetian Republic.

A Dream Abandoned

The eyes of the group were still on Jerusalem, but not for much longer. They would soon have to give up all hope of sailing to their longed-for destination. The Venetians had formed an alliance with Pope Paul III and the Emperor Charles V against the Turks, bringing to a standstill all sea voyages for Christian pilgrims to Jerusalem. The seas were deemed to be too dangerous because of the ever-present threat of encountering a Turkish fleet.

On 25 July, Ignatius, Favre and Laínez left Venice and set themselves up in the abandoned, half-ruined monastery of San Pietro in Vivarola, a short distance outside the walls of Vicenza in northern Italy. There they spent forty days living hidden, solitary lives, free from all external commitments, 'intent on nothing but their prayers'.[51] The other companions went to other towns throughout the region, also spending long periods in prayer while engaging in some priestly ministry.

Ignatius spoke of these days in Vivarola as his 'second Manresa'. He experienced 'many spiritual visions and consolations' at this time, though we are not told explicitly of what these visions and consolations consisted. Ignatius imagined that he found himself standing before the 'poor Christ', who called him to follow him in the highest spiritual poverty, and 'even in actual poverty, in insults and wrongs'.[52] At Vivarola, Ignatius asked the poor Christ that he might follow him under his standard, and prayed to the Blessed Virgin that she would place him with her Son.[53] He prayed that he would be a true companion of Jesus, sharing his lot.

Before the first companions dispersed throughout the Venetian Republic they agreed that if asked the name of the body to which they belonged they would answer that they were 'companions of Jesus', and that their sole superior was Christ. Ignatius was absolutely certain: their company could bear only *one* name. It would be the Compañia de Jesús, the union in companionship of those men chosen by God to serve and imitate the crucified Christ as their model and leader. Here, in Vivarola, is the origin of the naming of the Company of Jesus (or the Society of Jesus as it is known in the English-speaking world today).[54]

At the beginning of autumn, Xavier, Laínez, Bobadilla and Codure said their first Masses in the Church of San Pietro in Vivarola; Rodgrigues would say his first Mass in Ferrara. Ignatius postponed his first Mass to a later date.

Eventually, the companions moved beyond the Venetian Republic to the university cities of Padua, Ferrara, Bologna, Siena and Rome, where they hoped young men would join them. They began to preach in the city squares, calling people together by waving their hats around. In doing this, they showed remarkable courage since they did not know much Italian. They must have caused both edification and some amusement!

CHAPTER 9

Rome

U nable to realise their dream of travelling to the Holy Land, the companions decided to offer their services to Pope Paul III, as agreed in Montmartre, since he would surely know the greater needs of the universal Church. The first to arrive in Rome were Ignatius, Favre and Laínez.

La Storta

At the little village of La Storta, some twelve miles from Rome, on the Via Cassia, stood a half-ruined chapel. As Ignatius entered the chapel in early November 1537, he was filled with an overwhelming desire to obtain from God the favour for which he had prayed since his early days at Manresa. He had prayed to Our Lady to place him with her Son, Jesus, to be received under the standard of the Cross, and to be totally accepted into his companionship. We are told in *The Autobiography* that at La Storta 'he sensed such a change in his soul, and he saw so clearly that God the Father was putting him with Christ, his Son, that he would not have the wilfulness to have any doubt about this: it could only be that God the Father was putting him with his Son'.[55]

Pedro de Ribadaneira, in his life of Ignatius, tells us that 'he saw clearly how God the Father commended Ignatius and his companions in a loving way to God the Son as he was carrying the cross, and put them under the protection of his invincible right hand. When Jesus had most graciously received them, turning to Ignatius with a mild and untroubled expression, even while he was with the cross, he said, "I will be favourable to you in Rome." Ignatius was indescribably consoled by this marvellous divine vision.'[56]

After this mystical experience of La Storta, Ignatius is reported to have said to his companion, Diego Laínez, who was the principal witness of this event, 'What lies ahead of us in Rome I have no idea, whether God wants us to be put on a cross or on the wheel. But this I have discovered and know for sure: whatever outcome awaits us, Jesus Christ is going to be favourable to us.'[57] On entering Rome, Ignatius saw in advance that 'a terrible storm' was looming over himself and his companions. He is reported as saying to them, 'I see all doors shut; some great storm in a bad season has been prepared for us. But we are relying on Jesus; he will be favourable to us.'[58] After the vision of La Storta, Ignatius had an absolute certainty about the protection of the crucified Jesus, but was unsure how this would manifest itself.

Welcome in Rome

One immediate sign of the Lord's favour was the reception Ignatius received from Dr Pedro Ortiz. As soon as he arrived in Rome, Ortiz asked Ignatius himself to guide him through the Spiritual Exercises. What a change had come over him! He and Ignatius retired to the Benedictine monastery of Monte Cassino, where they spent forty days engaged in the full Spiritual Exercises. Ortiz would speak afterwards about the tremendous favour he had received from Ignatius.

Pedro Ortiz gained access to Pope Paul III once again for Ignatius, Favre and Laínez. The pope unexpectedly appointed Laínez and Favre as lecturers in theology at the University of Rome, the Sapientia, while Ignatius continued to guide people through the Spiritual Exercises. Among the most important of these individuals was Cardinal Gasparo Contarini, who would soon be the key figure in winning papal approval for the new Society of Jesus.

Gradually, the rest of the early companions began to drift into Rome, and they were soon preaching and teaching catechism in Spanish and in faulty Italian. They went begging in the streets, both for themselves and for the poor. Soon the people of Rome began to refer to them as 'pilgrim priests' or 'reformed priests', so impressed were they by the sincerity and pastoral zeal of these first companions.

CHAPTER 10

Foundation of the Society of Jesus

I gnatius's premonition of storm clouds looming in Rome was to prove all too accurate. Once again, some malicious rumours began to spread among the powerful Spanish community in Rome about the companions and about the Spiritual Exercises. The companions were accused of being *alumbrados*, or even Lutherans in disguise.

Challenging False Rumours
Ignatius, as usual, insisted that the matter be brought to court and a definitive judicial sentence delivered. When he saw that the judges were shying away from making a formal declaration about the case, in the course of the summer of 1538 he requested an audience with Pope Paul III at his summer residence at Frascati outside Rome. He told the pope openly about his past troubles with the Inquisition, how often he had been in prison and in chains and for what reasons. Ignatius writes a fascinating account of these 'malicious rumours' to his early benefactress, Isabel Roser, in a letter dated 19 December 1538, outlining for her the troubles the early companions endured in Rome.[59]

> For full eight months we experienced the severest opposition or persecution that we have ever experienced in this life …
> By spreading rumours and calling us unheard-of names, they were making us suspect and hateful to people, causing great

scandal, so that we were forced to present ourselves before the legate and governor of the city (for the Pope had then gone to Nice) ... We began by naming and summoning some who were behaving outrageously against us, so that they might declare before our superiors the evils they found in our life and teaching ...[60]

All of [our accusers] being curial officials and men of affairs, they raised such a stir among cardinals and many other persons of importance in the curia that they made us spend a great deal of time in this conflict ... At last two of the most important of them, having been summoned, appeared before the legate and the governor and declared that they had heard our sermons and lectures, etc. and had found everything, both in our teaching and in our lives, in entire justification of us ... We kept repeatedly asking, as we deemed was right, that whatever was evil or good in our teaching might be set forth in writing so that the scandal given to the people might be lifted; but we were never able to obtain this, either through justice or through law ...

A friend of ours spoke to the Pope after his return from Nice ... I talked with His Holiness alone in his room for an entire hour. Speaking to him there at length about our plans and intentions, I clearly related to him all the times when trials had been held against me in Spain and in Paris, and also the time when I had been imprisoned in Alcalá and Salamanca. I did this so that no one would be able to tell him more than I did ... I petitioned His Holiness ... for our teaching and behaviour to be investigated and examined by an ordinary judge whom His Holiness might commission: if they found evil, we wanted to be corrected and punished; if good, we wanted His Holiness to favour us. The Pope ... gave strict orders that the governor, who is a bishop and the chief justice of the city ... should inquire immediately into our case. He carried out a new trial and did so with diligence; moreover, the Pope, frequently speaking publicly in our favour and before our Society when he came to Rome (for every two weeks the fathers regularly go to hold a disputation during His Holiness' meal), has dispelled much of the tempest ... In my judgement things are going much better as we wish for the service and praise of God our Lord.[61]

Ignatius was always adamant that any accusation against his own teaching or the teaching of the early companions would be thoroughly investigated and found to be according to the official teaching of the Church. He did this to prevent any scandal attaching to the companions and to safeguard the faithful from any confusion in their faith.

Settling in Rome

Even though Ignatius had been ordained priest in June 1537, he postponed saying his first Mass for a year and a half. This is hardly conceivable today, but Ignatius had originally hoped to be able to celebrate his first Mass in the Holy Land. Since, as we saw, his plan to travel to the Holy Land had been frustrated, on Christmas Eve 1538 he celebrated his first Mass in the Basilica of Santa Maria Maggiore at the altar which, according to pious tradition, was said to enshrine the original manger of Bethlehem. This place was a symbolic substitution for the Holy Land.

That same winter Rome was afflicted by severe cold and famine. The early companions opened their residence to the people of Rome. This house belonged to a friend, Antonio Frangipani, and was not far from the Capitol. They remained in this residence from October 1538 until February 1541. At one time between 200 to 300 people were cared for during the city's crisis. Cardinals and curial officials followed the example of the companions by opening their residences to the poor, the cold and the destitute.

As in this instance, Ignatius did not confine his work to the house. He established a foundation for Roman orphans next to the church of Santa Maria in Aquiro at the end of the fearful winter of 1539. He organised an association of lay people – a confraternity – to run the house.[62] He also established a house for 'fallen women', the House of St Martha. Ignatius often preached to these women with great warmth of feeling. In the course of one year, eighty-three women were taken into the house. Later, similar houses were established in large Italian cities, including Bologna, Modena, Messina and Palermo. All these houses were run by charitable confraternities and received the necessary finance from generous nobles and wealthy citizens.

Many of the early Jesuits in Rome visited the infirm in the hospitals. These were mostly very squalid institutions, providing primitive medical care. One curious item that Ignatius promoted was the expansion of a much earlier papal decree of Innocent III, who was pope from 1130 to 1143. This decree, *Cum infirmitas corporis*, had fallen into disuse but was reinstated through the apostolic letters of Pope Paul III. According to its terms, doctors of the body were not to visit sick people until doctors of the soul had freed them from their sins through confession. Doctors had coat pockets filled with written testimonials that sick people had confessed to a priest, a practice that seems bizarre in the twenty-first century.

A Roman gentleman, Leonardo Bini, once recalled seeing Ignatius teaching catechism at the corner of the Via dei Banchi by the banks of the Tiber while street urchins threw bad apples at him. Young Pedro de Ribadeneira, who, as a teenager, came to live in the same house as Ignatius in Rome, tells us that Ignatius took up teaching the rudiments of Christian doctrine and the education of children in the faith. Quite a large number of people came every day to hear him speak, many men and women among them, some educated and some not. Though Ignatius spoke devotionally rather than learnedly, and though he used words that were unpolished and incorrect, he still moved the hearts of his audience.[63] Ribadeneira confides in his reader, 'I began to make notes of the mistakes he was making in Italian. Finally, so many were cropping up that I came to the conclusion that not some section but the entire speech had to be thoroughly purged of Hispanicisms.'[64]

During the period when Ignatius was teaching catechism in his execrable Italian at his favourite pitch in the Campo di Fiori, a young Florentine youth, Philip Neri,[65] was a frequent visitor to his rooms. Although he was not yet a priest, Philip was a true apostle of Rome and Ignatius delighted in his joyous company. Philip was twenty-five years younger than Ignatius. He was ordained in 1551 and lived in community with other priests in the Via di Montserrato in the church of San Girolamo della Carità, where he held his prayer meetings, often graced with the music of his famous friend, Giovanni Pierluigi da Palestrina (1525–94). He would go on to found the Congregation of the Oratory, or the Oratorians, in 1575.

Ignatius and the companions had still not abandoned altogether their hope of going to the Holy Land. According to a much later account by one of the early companions, Nicolás Bobadilla, Pope Paul III, during a theological disputation that Pierre Favre and Diego Laínez were holding at the papal dinner table, reproached them for this wish by saying that they could just as well help souls where they were; Rome could be their Jerusalem.[66] 'Why do you have such a great desire to go to Jerusalem?' the pope is reported as saying. 'Italy is a true and excellent Jerusalem if you wish to reap a harvest in God's Church.' With this admonition, the companions had to pray and reflect upon their future plans once again.

Papal Approval

The early companions had a series of meetings between March and June 1539, culminating in the drafting of what was entitled *The Five Chapters*. That document is the substantial draft of what came to be known as the *Formula of the Institute,* which is basically the Rule of the new Society of Jesus. Cardinal Contarini brought this document to Pope Paul III for his approval, with his own endorsement: 'The Spirit of God is here.'[67] The pope was reported to be 'much pleased' with it.

However, strong objections were raised in the Vatican Curia concerning this new Rule. Some members objected to the proposal to abolish the singing of the divine office in choir, since this was the practice in all other religious orders. Some were concerned about the abolition of cloister and the absence of a distinctive habit. Some asked the precise meaning of a vow to obey the pope 'concerning missions', as outlined in *The Five Chapters*, since all religious were expected to obey the pope, thus rendering this vow superfluous in their eyes. Others argued that there were already far too many religious orders, and that new ones had already been forbidden as far back as the Fourth Lateran Council in 1215.

Notwithstanding these curial objections, Paul III confirmed *The Five Chapters* by making them the substance of a papal bull. *Regimini militantis Ecclesiae* was issued from the Palazzo San Marco off the Piazza Venezia on 27 September 1540. This papal bull solemnly confirmed the foundation of the Society of Jesus, but limited the number of professed – or fully fledged – members to sixty. This severe restriction on membership was later lifted by the papal bull of Pope Julius III, *Iniunctum nobis*, published on 14 March 1544. With Paul III's bull came the recognition of the authority of a future superior general to write constitutions for this new religious order, helped by the views of his companions and based on the majority of votes.

Even before the deliberations of the first companions that produced *The Five Chapters*, the companions were receiving new members into their ranks. Before the papal bull was published, the Society had grown substantially and already numbered around twenty. The new members were Spanish, French and Italian, varied in their social backgrounds, but drawn almost exclusively from an academic elite.

In 1539, while the companions were still in the Frangipani house, the first Italian joined the Society. He was Pietro Codacio, a Lombard who had been ordained priest in 1532. Codacio had held the post of chamberlain in the Roman Curia. He was influential in effecting the transfer to the Society of the Church of Santa Maria della Strada in the centre of Rome, the first church ever held by the Jesuits. The church no longer exists, but the magnificent baroque Church of the Gesù was built on its site.

The First Superior General

On 8 April 1541, an election was held to choose the first superior general of the new order. By this time Francis Xavier had already set sail for India, but he had been invited to cast his vote before leaving. Ignatius was elected by unanimous consent of all the companions, both present and absent, with one exception. The exception was Ignatius himself. He begged his companions to think and vote again, because he was too conscious of his bad habits, his sins, past and present, and his other failings. Pedro de Ribadeneira reports what Ignatius said to his companions on learning of the result:

> Brothers, I am neither worthy of this office nor really suitable
> to direct others: how am I going to direct anyone else when I
> do not know how to direct myself? Truly and sincerely before
> our Lord and God, when I consider, when I carefully reflect
> on the waywardness of my past life and the sins of my pres-
> ent one and my many troubles, I cannot bring myself to take
> on myself that task you are imposing on me. For this reason,
> I ask that you be open to what I am saying: start afresh, and
> fervently commend to God the entire matter for three or four
> days, so that the divine inspiration and influence might lead
> us to select from our group precisely the right father who will
> best govern our whole Society.[68]

Reluctantly the companions agreed to a second ballot. After an inter-
val of three days, they reconvened, but by the same consensus Ignatius
was again elected general superior.

In search of an escape, Ignatius said he would leave the decision to
his confessor. He spent the last three days of Holy Week 1541 preparing
a general confession of his entire life, and on Holy Saturday confessed
to Teodoro de Lodi, a saintly and prudent Franciscan at the convent of
San Pietro in Montorio on the Janiculum Hill. Only when this good friar
told Ignatius that he would be resisting the Holy Spirit if he continued
to refuse did he eventually surrender. To everyone's delight, Ignatius
finally accepted the office of superior general. He was now fifty years
old. It was 19 April 1541.

Three days later, on 22 April, the six companions who were present
in Rome left for the Basilica of St Paul Outside-the-Walls to make their
solemn profession, taking vows of poverty, chastity and obedience.
Ignatius celebrated the Mass. At the moment before communion
Ignatius, holding the host in one hand and the formula of his vows in
the other, pronounced his vows and received communion. Then, with
five hosts on the paten, he received the professions of Jean Codure,
Paschase Broët, Diego Laínez, Alfonso Salmerón and Claude Le Jay.

After taking on the role of superior general, Ignatius went to the
kitchen and there, for a good length of time, he took on the role of cook!

Attitude to the Jews

Ignatius, on several occasions, expressed a wish to be of Jewish blood so as to be of the same race as Christ.[69] This left the Spaniards in particular among his listeners astounded, if not shocked, since anti-semitism was rife among them at that time. To them, it was unthinkable that anyone could wish to be Jewish.

In those days, Jews lived in ghettos in the city of Rome. Christians believed that it was their solemn duty to convert as many Jews as possible from Judaism to Christianity, since this was believed necessary for the salvation of their souls. As a man of his time, Ignatius too was keen on active proselytism among the Jews. To make it easier for Jews to become Christians, he acquired two houses in Rome for Jewish catechumens, one for men, the other for women. For this acquisition, he obtained the help of Margarita of Austria, the unhappily married daughter of the Emperor Charles V.[70]

A good number of converts from Judaism to Christianity were fed and instructed in these houses. Not a few Jews and Turks were baptised in the houses accommodating the catechumens. Ignatius was largely responsible for Paul III's bull *Cupientes iudaeos*, dated 21 March 1542, which decreed that Jewish converts to Christianity would not lose any of their property, even that obtained by usury. Until this time, converted Jews had to turn over all their fortune to the tax collectors, and they lost all their hereditary rights. Later, however, Pope Julius III (1550–55) and Pope Paul IV (1555–59) insisted that each Jewish synagogue in Rome contribute ten ducats per annum to these houses of catechumens. The Jewish community naturally resented this. Nevertheless, the idea of a *casa dei catecumeni* was exportable, and similar institutions opened in Venice, Bologna, Ferrara and Padua.

In 1551, the first converted Jew entered the Society of Jesus, admitted by Fr André des Freux. Still only twenty years old, Giovanni Battista Eliano (1530–89) had long been familiar with the Hebrew of the Old Testament, and also spoke Spanish, German and Turkish, in addition to his native Italian. In 1561, Pope Pius IV sent him to work with the Copts in Egypt. On his return to Rome he worked as a translator, and became especially notable for his translation of the decrees of the Council of Trent and for two catechisms that he translated into Arabic.

The Novices

Even though Ignatius did not bear the title of master of novices, he personally oversaw the formation of the new members of this new Society of Jesus. The novices in Rome, besides making the Spiritual Exercises, were sent to tend to the sick in the hospitals, to beg for alms in the streets and to preach at street intersections. They did this in order to overcome vanity and any undue solicitude for their honour. Each novice was also sent on a pilgrimage 'made on foot and without money, putting all hope in the Creator and Lord and accepting sleeping poorly and eating badly, because it seems to us that one who cannot live and walk for a day without eating or sleeping poorly cannot preserve long in our Society.'[71]

What Ignatius looked for in each novice was a spirit that was both docile and unattached to his own will. He expected every novice to have an upright and good intention. He preferred candidates who were active and hardworking. He respected the different temperament of each man. His policy with the novices was 'little by little'. He could combine gentleness with severity, being especially gentle towards the sick and those who were in the throes of temptation.[72] Ribadeneira tells us that Ignatius's principal method was 'to gain the man's heart by a very supportive, gentle, fatherly love because he was, indeed, a father to all of his sons'.[73] Echoing St Paul to the Corinthians, Ribadeneira says, 'To those who were infants in the way of virtue, he gave milk; to those who were making progress he gave bread with crusts; and those who had reached a certain degree of advancement he treated with greater rigour so that they would run at full speed toward perfection.'[74] It seems that Ignatius valued joyful generosity highly in the new recruits. He once told an ever-smiling Flemish novice, Frans de Coster, 'Laugh, my son, and be joyful in the Lord, for a religious has no reason to be sad and has a thousand reasons to rejoice.'[75]

The Episode of Isabel Roser

Isabel Roser had been a very generous benefactress of Ignatius, both during his time in Barcelona and, later, during his studies in Paris. In a letter of 19 December 1538, Ignatius acknowledges his indebtedness to Isabel: 'If I were to forget what I owe to our Lord through your hands, with such sincere love and inclination, I believe that his Divine Majesty would not be mindful of me; for you have always been so active on my behalf out of love and reverence for him.'[76]

In 1541, Isabel's husband died. The following year, she wrote to Ignatius telling him of her wish to live and work in Rome under his obedience. Ignatius responded to Isabel that some discernment was in order: was this a good or an evil spirit at work prompting her to such a desire? Nothing daunted, Isabel set out for Rome, accompanied by her servant, Francisca de Cruyllas, and her friend, Isabel de Josas. The ladies eventually arrived in Rome, followed by a whole shipload of chests and boxes. Initially, they settled at a private house with a Jesuit brother, Esteban de Eguía, as their servant.

Ignatius put Isabel to work in the house for prostitutes, the Casa Santa Marta. Soon, she and Francisca Cruyllas were joined by Lucrezia di Bradine, a Roman noblewoman. Isabel de Josas seems to have dropped out of the picture soon after their arrival in Rome.

Isabel Roser was obviously a lady of some influence in Roman society, because she was able to petition Paul III 'to be admitted to the least Society of Jesus' and that Ignatius be compelled to receive her. She wrote to the pope about her devotion to Ignatius and his work, and requested that she make solemn vows in the Society of Jesus.

On Christmas Day 1545, Isabel Roser, along with Lucrezia de Bradine and Francisca Cruyllas, professed vows of poverty, chastity and obedience. Isabel then bequeathed her entire estate to the Society, although Ignatius attempted to refuse it. Subsequently, when Ignatius was ill, Isabel insisted on attending to his needs. Her presence in the Jesuit house was overbearing at times, and was the cause of some disquiet and tension; they were human after all! At one point Isabel created another disturbance, when she invited two of her nephews to come to Rome so that she could arrange a marriage for one of them –

hardly a priority for the Jesuits!

It soon became clear that this experiment was a failure. In April 1546 Ignatius asked Paul III for permission to release the women from obedience to him. A formal petition followed in May 1547. With the authorisation of Pope Paul III, one of the early Jesuits, Jerónimo Nadal, in the presence of a lawyer, read a declaration to Isabel freeing her and her two lady companions from all previous commitments to and any ties with the Society of Jesus.

Understandably, Isabel was upset initially. She presented Ignatius with a detailed list of her gifts to the Society, demanding repayment. Ignatius responded with a bill of charges due to the Society, depicting Isabel as indebted to the Jesuits by some 150 ducats! The whole affair had tainted Ignatius's reputation, however, and in typical fashion he insisted that the false statements Isabel had been making be publicly adjudicated. The dispute went to court, where one of Isabel's nephews, Dr Francisco Ferrer, testified that Ignatius had been plotting the theft of his aunt's fortune all along! The judgment, however, was in Ignatius's favour, and Isabel signed an affidavit to the effect that any gifts she had given to the Society had been freely given. Prior to her return to Barcelona, Isabel and Ignatius were reconciled and their subsequent correspondence remained gracious.

Isabel later entered a Franciscan convent, where she died at the end of 1554. Lucrezia di Bradine eventually entered a convent in Naples, and Francisca Cruyllas spent the rest of her life working in the Hospital of the Cross in Barcelona.

CHAPTER 11

Scattering of the Companions

In 1541, Alfonso Salmerón and Paschase Broët were sent to Ireland as papal envoys at the request of the Archbishop of Armagh, Robert Wauchope, who had fled to the Continent rather than accept Henry VIII's supremacy of the Church in Ireland. Little was known about Ireland at the time, except that it was experiencing great turmoil, both religious and political. The mission of the two Jesuits was to sustain the faith of the faithful, reconcile the lapsed and report back to Rome about the true situation.

Mission to Ireland

Before travelling to Ireland, Ignatius gave instructions to Salmerón and Broët, including this piece of advice: 'Imitate the artifices of the evil spirit when he is tempting a good man: enter the other's door and come out your own in order to net him for the greater service of God.'[77]

The primate of Scotland, Cardinal David Beaton, whom Salmerón and Broët met in Lyons, told them that the Irish 'were the wildest people in the world, barbarous and incapable of any civilization'.[78] Four years later, Beaton was hacked to death in his bedroom by his own countrymen. They were indeed bloody and dangerous times!

Undeterred by Beaton's warnings, Salmerón and Broët, crossing over from Scotland, eventually arrived in the north of Ireland. They remained for thirty-four days. Without any knowledge of Irish or English, their ability to communicate with the native Irish was extremely limited. Danger was everywhere, and since they could not hide safely they decided there was no point in waiting for arrest: 'Our consciences told us not to run the risk of probable death without hope of doing any good.' They crossed back to Scotland and then travelled on to Dieppe, and thus reached Italy. Salmeron would later write, 'Ireland was not without its share of the cross of Christ our Lord for we suffered hunger and thirst, and had no place to put our heads, nor even a place to say an Our Father in peace.'[79]

Mission to the Indies

If the brief Irish mission had little success, the same could not be said of an earlier mission to the far-off Indies, made in response to the persistent request of King John III of Portugal for Jesuits to be sent to his territories in India. Initially, Ignatius designated Simão Rodrigues and Nicolás Bobadilla for the mission, but in the event neither of them made it. Bobadilla, who had been working in Naples, became ill on his arrival in Rome and was unable to depart for Lisbon. Rodriguez arrived safely in Lisbon, but was detained by King John at the royal court before he could set sail for Goa.

Ignatius was faced with a serious problem because of Bobadilla's illness. With only a day's warning, in March 1540, Ignatius notified Francis Xavier, who had no inkling of any change of plan, that he would have to undertake this mission to the Indies in place of Bobadilla. The announcement brought Xavier great joy, for he had long had an intense desire to convert the Gentiles.[80] After a delay of some nine months in Lisbon, on 7 April 1541 Xavier set out for Goa. An Italian Jesuit, Messer Paulo, embarked with him. The pair eventually arrived safely in Goa in the spring of 1542, having spent the winter in Mozambique. Xavier pronounced his final vows in Goa in 1543, separated by thousand of miles from his early companions.

Francis Xavier's letters from the Indies proved to be most effective propaganda for the Society of Jesus in Europe, and were read with interest and enthusiasm in the royal courts of Spain and Portugal, as they were in Paris and Cologne and later at the Council of Trent (1545–63).

They were copied and re-copied, and were the source of inspiration for many generous young men to follow in Xavier's missionary footsteps.

Xavier laboured tirelessly in the East (mostly in India and Japan) for a number of years and then, in 1552, he courageously set out for China, accompanied by a Jesuit scholastic named Ferreira and a Chinese layman named Antonio. He was sick, emaciated and exhausted when he reached the island of Shangchuan, from where he hoped to sail to the mainland. He died one night in early December 1552. Some Portuguese merchants who were present at his death wrapped his corpse, whole and entire, in the religious garb he wore, covered it in lime and buried it in the ground. Their intention was to carry the bones back to India after the lime had consumed the rest, as Xavier himself had requested. After three months, the grave was dug up and Xavier's clothing was found to be entirely intact; his body was quite solid and incorrupt. His body was then brought back to Goa, where it was embalmed and placed in the college chapel in the presence of the local dignitaries and the citizenry. The people of Goa greatly venerated Xavier, and his place of rest quickly became a place of pilgrimage. Shortly after Xavier's death, King John III of Portugal ordered the beginning of his canonisation process, and he was canonised on 12 March 1622, along with Ignatius.

We still possess some of the correspondence between Ignatius and Xavier. Xavier used to sign his letters to Ignatius, 'Your least son in the farthest exile'.

Xavier's letters would sometimes take two years to arrive in Rome, and it was almost a miracle that they arrived at all. In the end, Ignatius called Xavier back to Rome so that he could learn at first hand about the problems the Society was facing in far-off Asia. Ignatius's summons arrived two years after Xavier had died.

Taking Root in Spain

The Society took rather longer to establish itself in Spain than in the Italian peninsula. This was mainly due to the fierce opposition raised by Melchor Cano, the brilliant Dominican theologian of Salamanca. Cano disapproved strongly of some of the novelties in the Jesuit way of proceeding and even went so far as to suggest that the

Spiritual Exercises were heretical in their teaching.

In stark contrast, Francis Borgia,[81] the Duke of Gandia, requested permission to join the Society soon after becoming a widower. His eminence in Spanish royal circles meant that the matter had to be kept secret. Through his father he was the great-grandson of Cardinal Rodrigo Borgia, later Pope Alexander VI, and the grand-nephew of the famous Lucrezia Borgia, wife to seven husbands. On 2 February 1548, Francis Borgia made his solemn profession of vows in secret. He subsequently came to Rome during the final months of 1550.

The Spiritual Exercises

In 1548, Paul III appointed three experts to examine the *Spiritual Exercises*: the Inquisitor Cardinal of Burgos, the Vicar of the Supreme Pontiff, Fillippo Archinto, and Egidio Foscharari, who was Master of the Sacred Palace. They approved them with a laudatory testimonial. On 31 July 1548, Paul III issued the papal bull *Pastoralis officii*, confirming and approving the *Spiritual Exercises*. They had been translated into elegant Latin from the original Spanish by Jesuit André des Freux in 1546–47.

During Ignatius's life, the full Spiritual Exercises – a retreat of some thirty days – was given to approximately 7,500 people, of whom about 1,500 were women, including religious sisters. Of the 6,000 or so men who made the full Exercises, only about 1,000 were members of religious orders or became religious afterwards. The majority were laymen who continued on in their chosen state of life. It is believed that there were about 100 Jesuits giving the Exercises in more than 100 towns and cities in the years 1540–56.

The Schools

In the years 1548 and 1549, the Jesuits began a totally new work, a work for which they would subsequently become famous down through the centuries: education. The first Jesuit schools were founded in Messina and Palermo in Sicily, and rapidly spread to numerous towns and cities, not only in Europe but also in Latin America and Asia. It has often been said that the Jesuits became 'the schoolmasters of Europe'.

Schools very quickly became the chief work of the Society of Jesus, with parents anxious that there should be a Jesuit school in their town or city. From approximately 1551, the Jesuits began to open schools at the rate of about four or five per year. By 1565 they had thirty colleges in Italy alone. This rapid expansion became a great drain on manpower in the early Society, but the Jesuits were anxious to educate good Christian leaders for the future. The education was free of charge 'for rich and poor', the cost of the whole enterprise being borne by wealthy nobles and benefactors.[82] The schools looked more to the formation of mind and character than to the mere acquisition of knowledge. It was hoped that students would become active and committed Christians in the service of the common good, and especially the less fortunate members of Society.

Ignatius, while preoccupied with the rapidly growing Society, still had time to keep an eye on aspects of the curriculum taught in these schools. Jesuit schools became renowned for their high academic standards and for their promotion of music and theatre, the students often giving public performances of Greek and Latin plays and orchestral pieces to the citizenry of the towns and cities

Ignatius would not permit a Jesuit to administer any sort of physical punishment in the colleges, not even on the palm of the hand. A lay corrector was appointed to administer any such punishment to the boys. This arrangement had some unfortunate consequences for the lay corrector at the hands of some irate students!

In February 1551, Francis Borgia, with Ignatius's encouragement and advice, founded a college in Rome. This became known as the Roman College, and later as the Gregorian University, and won renown throughout the Catholic world for its scholarship and research. Young Jesuits from sixteen or more different countries, all speaking different languages, attended this college. In such a Tower of Babel, it was just as well that the language of instruction was Latin for all.

Resignation Offered and Rejected

In 1550, Ignatius called a meeting, summoning to Rome from the various provinces all the first fathers who could attend without inconvenience or interruption to their work. At this meeting, he handed each of them a letter written in his own hand in Spanish.

> Upon examining the matter factually and, so far as I could perceive within myself, without any emotional bias, I have come on many and varied occasions to the factual conclusion that because of my many sins, many imperfections, and many inward and outward infirmities, I lack to an almost infinite degree the qualities required for the responsibility over the Society which I presently hold by the Society's appointment and imposition ... All this being taken into account, in the name of the Father and of the Son and of the Holy Spirit, my one God and Creator, I lay down and resign, simply and absolutely, the office I hold, requesting and with all my soul beseeching in our Lord the professed, along with whomever they shall prefer to add for this purpose, would accept this offering of mine, so justified before his Divine Majesty.[83]

In his biography of Ignatius, Pedro de Ribadeneira tells us that, while admiring Ignatius's humility, the Jesuits gathered in Rome for this meeting could not in good conscience agree to his request. They told Ignatius that they would not have another general superior while he was alive, and they asked him to retract his petition. Ribadeneira, in typical fashion, writes that those present told Ignatius that he was the father of the Society, that he was everybody's teacher and the leader chosen by God to lay the foundation for this spiritual building.[84] So, disappointed in his hope that he could lay aside the burden he was shouldering, and even though he was recovering from a recent illness, Ignatius concluded that it was God's will that he continue as superior general, and so gave his complete attention to governing the Society.

CHAPTER 12

Directing the Society of Jesus

Externally, Ignatius's life in Rome now seemed pedestrian and routine for the most part. Back in March 1541, even before the election of a superior general, the companions had entrusted to Ignatius and Jean Codure the task of studying the requirements for the new constitutions of the Society, and reporting to them at regular intervals on the work accomplished.[85] Ignatius and Codure set to work but Codure died suddenly on 29 August 1541. Ignatius was left alone to continue this burdensome work and, without Codure's support, he did not make great progress. He was in frail health and had many other preoccupations about the ever-growing young Society. Nevertheless, to the year 1545 belongs a document known as *Constitutiones circa missiones* (Constitutions about Missions) that would later form the substance of Part VII of the Constitutions. This early draft of 1545 tells us much about what Ignatius saw as a priority for the Society of Jesus: the mission on which each Jesuit was to be sent by virtue of his vow of obedience.

Composing the Constitutions

March 1547 saw the arrival in Rome of Juan Alfonso de Polanco and a new stage began in the work of the preparation and drafting of the Jesuit Constitutions.[86] Polanco made a thorough study of the constitutions and rules of older religious orders, including the Rules of Saints

Augustine, Basil, Benedict and Francis, as well as the ordinances of the Franciscans and Dominicans. Ignatius and Polanco also investigated the constitutions and ordinances of other institutions, including the more famous colleges of Europe, such as Alcalà, Paris, Louvain, Padua, Bologna and Salamanca. Polanco, who always considered himself to be the 'memory and hand' of Ignatius, worked tirelessly on this burdensome task. A preliminary draft of the constitutions was ready by September 1550.

Those who were available to come to Rome from among the early companions arrived in the winter of 1550–51 to examine the work thus far. They suggested certain emendations, and by April 1553 Ignatius and Polanco had put together a new text, which became known as the Autograph Text. It was given the force of law in the Society of Jesus in 1558, two years after Ignatius's death.

The Jesuit *Constitutions* is a unique document in this genre. They are divided into ten parts, following the path of a Jesuit's life from his first application to join the Society, through noviceship, the years of study, admission to full membership of the Society and personal life.[87] They then deal with the more corporate aspects of the Society: the choosing of missions, help towards maintaining unity in the widely scattered group, the character and leadership of the superior general and, finally, how the Society can best be preserved and developed.

The Constitutions declare that the end of the Society of Jesus is the salvation and perfection of its members and the salvation and perfection of others. The vows that a Jesuit takes of poverty, chastity and obedience and, in many cases, the fourth vow of special obedience to the pope in relation to missions, are a means to this end. Jesuits are to strive to seek God in all things, not just in prayer but also in their various apostolic works.

Interestingly, Ignatius, in Part IV of the *Constitutions* stipulates that there should be professors of Latin, Greek and Hebrew to help the Jesuit scholastics study the Old and New Testaments in their original languages.[88] Ignatius is showing great foresight here. To prepare Jesuits to go among the Muslims and the Turks, a knowledge of Arabic or Chaldaic would be expedient. Ignatius still had his eye on the Muslim world!

In what pertains to the vows, Ignatius calls the vow of poverty the 'mother', 'strong wall' and 'bulwark' of religious life.[89] Ignatius was only too aware of the scandal of opulence within the Church and wanted the Jesuits to live simply and frugally. They were not to demand any payment for Masses said or lectures given. The professed of four vows were to live totally on alms, without fixed income. All Jesuits were to be ready to beg from door to door when necessity required it. Ignatius wanted it to be seen and known that his followers sought nothing but the eternal salvation of people. Poverty was an unspoken sermon on the subject of trust in God. Ignatius made it absolutely clear in his letters that absence of funds was never an adequate reason to halt any apostolic work; even if money had to be borrowed, a start was to be made. He assured his secretary, Juan de Polanco, that the worst that could happen to the Jesuits was that they would land in jail for bad debts!

Today, we would find it strange that Ignatius devotes only a few lines to his treatment of the vow of chastity. We may even find his words shocking and naïve:

> What pertains to the vow of chastity does not require explanation, since it is evident how perfectly it should be preserved through the endeavour in this matter to imitate the angelic purity by the purity of the body and mind.[90]

The American Jesuit scholar George Ganss throws some light on this seemingly extraordinary statement of Ignatius. Ganss writes that the value of virginity as an ideal was accepted almost universally and without question in the Catholic countries of Europe in the 1500s, in spite of the many well-known lapses in its practice.[91] Even though some humanists and Protestants had attacked celibacy, the modern psychological interest in matters pertaining to sexuality, so widely discussed today, obviously had not then arisen. Ganss argues that it was natural for Ignatius, as for other spiritual writers of his age, to dismiss the vow of chastity with a brief remark. Ganss adds that we can safely conjecture that if Ignatius were alive today, he would be impelled to a fuller treatment of chastity by his sensitivity to contemporary needs and by his loyalty to the pope, the Church, the Second Vatican Council and the members of his order.

When treating of obedience, Ignatius desired that each Jesuit should distinguish himself in this virtue and he wrote several strongly worded letters on this topic. He was desirous that every Jesuit be available for mission, eager for service in the vineyard of the Lord, and ready to go wherever he might be sent.

Ignatius had great confidence in the wisdom of Jerónimo Nadal and his knowledge of the Society's affairs.[92] In order to promote the new Constitutions, he sent Nadal as his emissary to Sicily, Spain, Portugal, Germany, Austria and Italy to explain the content of the *Constitutions* to the various Jesuit communities that had sprung up. He gave Nadal many blank pages, to be used for both private letters and letters patent, each bearing Ignatius's own signature and stamped with the seal of the Society. On these blank pages, Nadal could write what he judged would be best in the particular circumstances of time and place.

The Case of Princess Juana

The Infanta Juana was the daughter of the Emperor Charles V and brother of Philip II of Spain. In 1552, at the age of seventeen, she was married to Prince João Manuel, the heir to the Portuguese throne. Two years after their marriage her husband died. Eighteen days later Juana gave birth to the future King Sebastian, who would later have Jesuit tutors. Philip appointed Juana regent of Spain, a post she held for five years, while he was in England and the Netherlands.

To the consternation of Ignatius and his companions, Juana let it be known in late 1554 that she herself was determined to become a Jesuit. The situation was delicate, since to refuse her request could have serious consequences for the work of the Society in Spain. The Jesuits debated the very special circumstances of 'Matteo Sanchez', the secret pseudonym they used in all correspondence about Juana and 'his' request to enter the Society. Ignatius allowed her to take the simple vows of a Jesuit scholastic.[93] This was kept secret even from her brother, King Philip II. Juana's life at court was one of unusual austerity. Her palace was said to be 'more like a convent' and she remained unfailingly helpful to the Society. In 1558, two years after the death of Ignatius, Francis Borgia wrote to the second superior general, Diego Laínez, 'She grows daily in the spiritual life and in pious submission to the Society; I think she is one of those who fully understands the nature of the Society, and she has in truth a good will for all our affairs.'[94] Juana died in 1573 at the age of thirty-eight, the only woman Jesuit.

The Spiritual Diary

Of all the personal diaries that Ignatius kept, only two small notebooks have survived. The first records his mystical experiences from 2 February to 12 March 1544, and the second similar experiences from 13 March 1544 to 27 February 1545. These notebooks, commonly known as the Spiritual Diary, were made available only from 1934.

All who were close to Ignatius in his Roman days and saw him at prayer are agreed that a deep personal sense of union with the Trinity was of the essence in his spiritual life. We see mention of the Trinity and of tears on almost every page of the diary. Also frequently mentioned is 'the gift of tears' during prayer, an experience regularly mentioned by saints and mystics like St Francis of Assisi and St Catherine of Siena. 'The most excellent tears,' Ignatius wrote to Francis Borgia on 28 September 1548, 'are those that come from the thought and love of the Divine Persons'.

These periods of illumination were punctuated at times with intervals of darkness and isolation. On 12 March Ignatius writes:

> After Mass and later in my room, I found myself completely bereft of all help, unable to find delight in the mediators, or in the Divine Persons; I felt as remote and separated from them as if I had never felt their influence in the past, or was ever to feel it in the future. Instead I was beset by thoughts, now against Jesus, now against another.[95]

After Mass, it was usual for Ignatius to remain at prayer for two hours. Though the Jesuit rule stipulated that there would be no sung office in the Society, Ignatius personally derived great comfort from the chant of the sung office, if he chanced to enter a church at Vespers or during some other ceremony.

The German College

Ignatius was anxious lest the rapidly increasing numbers joining the Society might lead to a lowering of standards, and was convinced it needed a superior general in good health to watch over its expansion. As we have seen, however, his proffered resignation was twice rejected.

Ignatius had learned over the years about the activities of the Protestant reformers, and the separation of much of northern Europe, especially Germany, from the Roman Catholic Church. To help counteract this movement, Pope Julius III founded the German College in Rome on 31 August 1551. This new institution was to be governed by the Society of Jesus.

In 1552, Ignatius wrote to the Jesuits who were teaching in Vienna, Ingolstadt, Cologne and Louvain, bidding them to send young men between the ages of sixteen and twenty-two to Rome. All should be of agreeable appearance, physically healthy and capable of bearing up under the labour of study. They should be endowed with talent and be of upright character, so that one could reasonably hope that they would emerge as reliable and strenuous workers in the Lord's vineyard. The better educated were to be preferred, and special consideration should be given to those of noble blood, something that was much esteemed in those nations. He was hoping for promising young men who on their return would be promoted to bishoprics and important roles, and who could be trusted for their loyalty to Rome. This hope was realised before the end of the century, when most of the important bishoprics in central Europe were occupied by former students of the German College. To his last day, Ignatius struggled to maintain the financial viability of the German and Roman colleges, both of which he regarded as key to the future of Catholicism in Europe.

Jesuit Bishops?

As early as December 1546 Ignatius pointed out to Ferdinand I, King of Bohemia and younger brother of Charles V, that of the nine companions who were professed at that time, four or five had been presented for bishoprics. Ignatius resisted this vigorously. Writing to King Ferdinand, he makes his position quite clear.

We are convinced in conscience that for us to accept the prelacy would be to demolish the Society. Indeed, if I wanted to think or imagine a variety of methods for overthrowing and wrecking this Society, one of the most effective – indeed the most effective – would be to accept a bishopric. For us to abandon our simplicity would be for us to undo our spirit and so undo our profession, and its undoing would mean the complete ruin of the Society.[96]

A few years later, however, Ignatius softened his stance with regard to Jesuits accepting bishoprics. On that occasion, Jesuit Nuñes Barretto was consecrated Patriarch of Ethiopia in a grand ceremony in Lisbon, along with two auxiliary bishops, also Jesuits, Andres de Oviedo and Melchor Carneiro. Twelve priests were to accompany them to Ethiopia. Ignatius had long been fascinated by the stories of an ancient Christian civilisation in Ethiopia, and he hoped that this mission would forge new contacts and even bring about reconciliation. Since he regarded the assignment to Ethiopia to be one of unrelieved hardship, he had no difficulty in allowing his men to accept these bishoprics. Who would ambition them?

Today, there are about 100 Jesuit bishops in the world usually, though not always, in the Developing World, where the demands are greatest. One wonders what Ignatius would have thought of a Jesuit pope!

Inclusive Pastoral Concern

We would be shocked today to hear a Roman Catholic call a Lutheran or a Calvinist a 'heretic'. To do so would be an affront to our more developed theology and ecumenical sensitivities. But there was no ecumenical movement in Ignatius's time. Roman Catholics were convinced that theirs was the only true Church and that those reformers – whether they be Lutherans, Calvinists or Anabaptists – who had broken away from Rome were rightly branded as heretics. As a man of his time, Ignatius would have shared that view. Notwithstanding this widespread attitude, which often generated bitterness on both sides, Ignatius wrote to certain Jesuit theologians who were to work in the German lands giving them the following advice:

> You should attempt to win the friendship of any leading ad-
> versaries and of the influential among those who are heretics,
> or suspected of heresy, and are not altogether obdurate ...
> Your zeal in pursuing heresy should evidence above all love
> for the heretics' persons, desire for their salvation, and com-
> passion for them.[97]

The sincere pastoral concern and respect that Ignatius shows here for
the reformers was remarkable in those days. As with the reformers, Ignatius also encouraged friendly discussions with leading Muslims and
masters of the Quranic law. He asked that a copy of the Quran be sent
to him, and he encouraged Jesuits to make themselves familiar with its
theological terminology.

CHAPTER 13

Last Days and Death

In his last three years, during which he was often close to death, Ignatius spent a total of six months sick in bed. In moments of pain or anxiety, he would sometimes call Father André des Freux from the German College and ask him to play the clavichord for him, or he would ask a Jesuit brother to sing him a song to lift his spirits.

In later years, artists depicted Ignatius on his deathbed clutching a rather large crucifix, surrounded by his distraught Jesuit brothers. The reality was quite different. Ignatius's final illness started in the early summer of 1556. On 19 May, he wrote to a friend, Leonora Mascarena, 'This is the last letter that I will write to you; in a short time, I hope, I will be entreating the Lord more ardently on your behalf in heaven.'[98]

To avoid the overpowering heat of Rome, Ignatius went out to the country villa, a vineyard retreat, but since the heat there was also oppressive, he returned to Rome shortly afterwards, on 26 July. No one in the community was too disturbed when Ignatius took to his bed again. Two days later, on 28 July, he received communion instead of offering Mass himself. That too was not unusual at that time. In typical fashion, Ignatius was more concerned about Diego Laínez, who was down with a severe fever, and other members of the community who were also ill, than he was about himself.

On 30 July, at three o'clock in the afternoon, Ignatius called for his secretary, Juan de Polanco, and asked him to obtain a papal blessing both for himself and Laínez. Polanco was busy writing letters at the time and suggested that he would get the blessing the next day. Ignatius replied, 'I would prefer it done today, rather than tomorrow, or at least as soon as possible, but do what you think best.'[99] That evening, at dinner, Ignatius had discussions with Fathers Polanco and Madrid about a house they had recently purchased for the use of the Roman College.[100] Ignatius retired and did not summon anyone to come to his assistance during the night.

The next morning his Jesuit brothers realised that Ignatius was dying. Polanco rushed to the Vatican to obtain the papal blessing. When he returned, Ignatius was already dead. He died on 31 July 1556, 'earlier than two hours before sunlight'. He was in his sixty-sixth year. That same afternoon, at about two o'clock, Renaldo Colombo, a surgeon who held the chair of anatomy in Padua University, performed an autopsy on Ignatius's body. He found stones in the portal vein, into which they had passed from the gall bladder, a process that causes pain of the most acute kind.[101] Ignatius must have endured this excruciating pain regularly over the previous thirty years, when the attacks would have been a regular occurrence. When the autopsy was completed, the body was embalmed. A Jesuit, Jacopino del Ponte, made a portrait of Ignatius after his death, using Ignatius's death mask as a model.

The Jesuit Pedro de Ribadeneira tells us [102] that there was no image of Ignatius made from him during his life.

> Ignatius neither could endure having a portrait of himself painted or likeness made nor had any vanity or even the shadow of vanity ... Not a single one of us could be found who would dare to ask him to allow this. Without his knowledge, some such attempts were made, but without success. So the images that we have of him in circulation have been drawn from something fashioned after his death. In my opinion, the one that comes closest is that of a man especially outstanding for his portraits from life, Alfonso Sánchez, the painter of King Philip II.[103]

Ignatius's funeral was held on 1 August. Enormous crowds of ordinary people came, and huge numbers visited his grave. His body was buried on the left side of the main altar in the Church of Santa Maria della Strada. When this church was demolished, Ignatius's remains were transferred to the church that replaced it, the magnificent Church of the Gesù, where they are now enshrined.

Ignatius died in the thirty-fifth year after his conversion experience on his sickbed in Loyola. He left behind twelve established Jesuit provinces: Portugal, Castile, Andalusia, Aragon, Italy, Naples, Sicily, Upper Germany, Lower Germany, France, Brazil and East India. In these provinces there were almost a hundred colleges.[104] Of the 1,000 Jesuits at that time, only three per cent of them were solemnly professed of four vows.

Among those who petitioned the Holy See for Ignatius's beatification was Philip II of Spain. During the beatification process, some of the older fathers of the Society, who personally remembered Ignatius, gave their recollections of him. One recalled how Ignatius playfully pulled his ear; another how Ignatius gave him a fatherly hug; a third how Ignatius remained calm even when the street boys threw apples at him while Ignatius tried to teach them catechism. One said that no one enjoyed a well-aimed joke or a comical situation more than Ignatius himself; such occurrences were a *grande festa* for him.[105]

On 27 June 1609 Ignatius was beatified. Then, on 12 March 1622, he was canonised in company with Francis Xavier, Teresa of Avila, Philip Neri and an eleventh-century farmhand, Isidore, to whose intercession King Philip II had attributed his recovery from a serious illness. At the time of Ignatius's canonisation, the Society numbered more than 14,000, many of them in formation, spread across the whole world from China to Peru.

CHAPTER 14

Ignatius as Seen by Others

The second and third generations of Jesuits, in their profound admiration for Ignatius, were perhaps in danger at times of placing him on an unreal pedestal. Among the most influential of these Jesuits were Jerónimo Nadal and Pedro de Ribadeneira. Ribadeneira's Latin biography of Ignatius appeared in 1572, and according to St Peter Canisius (1521–97) it could not be recommended enough.[106] For his part, Nadal was adamant that Ignatius was the sole founder of the Society, a view not shared by some of the first companions themselves, notably Nicolás Bobadilla. Indeed, Ignatius himself had insisted that the early companions together were the founders of the Society, impelled by the inspiration of the Holy Spirit.

During the late sixteenth and early seventeenth centuries, many Baroque Jesuit churches were built in the cities of Europe, churches that are still standing to this day. The art of these buildings, with their ornate style, frequently stressed the glorified and celestial Ignatius. He is often depicted above the high altar in the sanctuary as being enthroned on a cloud in the heavens. The most famous examples of this kind of art can be seen in the two great Jesuit churches in Rome, the Church of the Gesù and the Church of St Ignatius, but they were widely copied elsewhere. It was during these same centuries that the image of Ignatius, the soldier of serene sanctity, was fashioned, even though Ignatius was never actually a professional soldier.

So, what was the real Ignatius like? What did others see in him? Was he universally admired? What did his critics say? We have already gleaned something of the character of the earlier Ignatius, from Loyola until his final arrival in Rome. This Ignatius was initially headstrong, vain and proud, but also courageous and imaginative. He gradually became more self-reflective, with a growing ability to understand himself and others. He seems to have had a capacity for deep and lasting friendships, and for earning the confidence of a wide range of people. There was something about this Ignatius that made people, both male and female, want to share his spiritual journey and enterprise. He seems to have had a remarkable capacity to understand people, to read their minds and their deeper desires, to direct them in their spiritual life, and to see their potential if only they would open themselves to the dream of God for them.

Through hours of prayer and fidelity, Ignatius grew to be a mystic. He had a deep personal relationship with Jesus Christ, rooted in experiences he alludes to but never really tries to describe. He also had a deep devotion to the Blessed Trinity, which frequently brought him to tears. His desire to follow in the footsteps of Jesus, to labour under the banner of Christ's Cross and to live a life of costly discipleship grew stronger as time went on. In Rome, he proved himself to be a very able and creative administrator, surrounding himself with some very talented Jesuits who helped him in the governance of the Society.

Ignatius was tenacious when he set his mind on something. Especially, he was determined that any accusations made against himself, his early companions or the later Society of Jesus – whether by the Inquisition or by other individuals, however powerful – should be investigated thoroughly, whatever the personal cost or inconvenience. It was vital to him, for the sake of his mission, that his own reputation and the reputation of those who shared his spiritual enterprise should be left unsullied.

One fascinating document, which gives an insight into the day-to-day life of Ignatius and the lives of those who shared the residence with him in Rome, is what is called the *Memoriale* of Luís Gonçalves da Câmara.[107] Da Câmara spent two years in Rome (1553–55) with Ignatius, and was convinced that future generations of Jesuits could learn much from what he had to tell of Ignatius and of life in the residence. While in Rome, da Câmara jotted down some notes in Castilian, although it was almost twenty years before he could turn his attention to them again. When he did so, and with the passing of time, he saw some things in a new light, and he felt the need to add further comments in Portuguese. He died in 1575 before he had completed the work. Da Câmara's text was sent to Rome at the request of the fourth superior general, Everard Mercurian, who must have deemed it unsuitable for publication. He consigned it to the Society's archives, where it remained until it finally emerged in the twentieth century. It was only in 2004 that the first English translation of da Câmara's work was published.[108]

Obviously, it is possible to touch on only a few brief points from Da Câmara's account here. Da Câmara tells us how he often came across Ignatius shut in his chapel in such devotion that this could be seen in his features. After saying his Mass, Ignatius remained in prayer for two hours. As regards spiritual reading, Ignatius told da Câmara that he had read *The Imitation of Christ* at Manresa, and that since then he never wished to read any other devotional book. Ignatius recommended it to all with whom he had dealings, and each day he read a chapter himself. A conversation with Ignatius was, according to da Câmara, like a reading of *The Imitation of Christ* put into practice.

Da Câmara notes that Ignatius's manner of living 'observes all the rules of the Spiritual Exercises exactly in such a way that he seems to have planted them in his soul'. Yet, as da Câmara also notes, Ignatius urged the need for flexibility in directing others, since 'it seemed to him there was no greater mistake in spiritual matters than wishing to govern others as one rules oneself'.

To da Câmara it seemed that everything Ignatius did was 'founded solely on trust in God … It appears that in whatever he undertakes, he has first negotiated it with God and, since we ourselves do not see that he has negotiated with God, we are appalled at what he takes on.' Da Câmara is here suggesting that Ignatius's decisions, made in the context of his personal relationship with God in prayer, enabled him to act with total confidence when undertaking even the most daring projects.

Surprisingly, perhaps, for someone who spent so much time in prayer himself, da Câmara remembers Ignatius saying that for a person who is truly mortified – meaning open to do the will of God – a quarter of an hour in prayer is enough to unite that person with God. In another place, da Câmara quotes Ignatius saying something we might find even stranger. Da Câmara insists that the Jesuit community heard Ignatius say many times that 'of a hundred people given to prayer, ninety were subject to illusions'. Da Câmara then adds, 'though I am not sure if he used to say ninety or ninety-nine'. Was Ignatius being a tinge humorous here? One can almost imagine him with a wise grin on his face.

Ignatius is often thought of as being very serious and strict, demanding of himself and of others. As we will see, there is some truth in this, but he was by no means devoid of a sense of humour. Da Câmara describes Ignatius as a 'tiny little Spaniard, a bit lame, with joyful eyes'. When he invited someone to stay with the community for lunch, he would say, according to Da Câmara, 'Sir, please stay with us, if you would like to do some penance'. Da Câmara also relates how greatly Ignatius enjoyed the company of the Jesuit brothers, especially those who were devout and lovers of obedience and holy simplicity. On the other hand, we are told that Ignatius could not abide it in conversation when someone spoke 'pompously or authoritatively', as though laying down the law. Da Câmara even tells a tale at his own expense. He admits that he often spoke too quickly. One day, Ignatius told him that it would be a good idea to have some bells attached to his ears, so that when he spoke he should be reminded by their ringing of his need to speak more slowly!

Da Câmara tells us that there were many things that fostered the love that his fellow Jesuits had for Ignatius. He mentions especially his 'great affability' and 'the great care which he took of everyone's health'. Ignatius was 'naturally the most courteous and considerate of men', and that showed itself particularly in his treatment of anyone going through a rough patch. Da Câmara mentions especially how gently Ignatius used to treat the novices, who were just beginning their Jesuit life. Ignatius gave 'help to the weak … in a spirit of gentleness'.

This picture of Ignatius, as conveyed in the *Memoriale*, is echoed in a letter of 29 July 1553, written by a young Jesuit, Frans de Costere, who had been sent from Cologne to Rome.

> The day before yesterday I saw for the first time, with indescribable joy and eagerness, the Reverend Father Ignatius. I could not see enough of him. For his countenance is such that one cannot look upon it long enough. The old man was walking in the garden, leaning on a cane. His face shone with godliness. He is mild, friendly, and amiable so that he speaks with the learned and unlearned, with important people and little people, all in the same way: a man worthy of all praise and reverence. No one can deny that a great reward is prepared for him in heaven for everything.[109]

Not everything in da Câmara's account, however, shows Ignatius as 'mild, friendly and amiable'. Most puzzling, perhaps, is Ignatius's treatment of some of his closest and most able associates, as reported by da Câmara. In general, we are told, 'our Father often leads his subjects along this road, that is to say, praising them for their good qualities and flattering them. It is surprising with what circumspection he treats any person whomsoever, unless it happens to be a Nadal or a Polanco; these he treats without any respect but rather harshly and with rigorous admonitions.' This is surely strange, considering that Jerónimo Nadal and Juan de Polanco were key collaborators of Ignatius. It is doubtful if Ignatius would ever have finished writing the Jesuit *Constitutions* without the scholarly and ever-faithful help of Polanco, secretary of the Society of Jesus. With regard to Nadal, as we have already seen, Ignatius sent him throughout Europe to explain the newly written *Constitutions* to the Jesuits scattered throughout these lands, and had chosen him as vicar general of the Society when he himself was gravely ill.

Another source also speaks of Ignatius's harsh behaviour towards his most trusted co-workers and intimates, Laínez, Nadal, de Polanco and also da Câmara himself.[110] Pedro de Ribadeneira, Ignatius's later official biographer, says of Polanco that he scarcely heard a good word during his nine years as secretary; Ignatius rebuked Nadal so much that he sometimes could not keep from crying; and Laínez, Ignatius's eventual successor as superior general, once complained to Ribadeneira, 'What have I done against the Society that this saint treats me in this way?'

It is not easy to explain any of this, especially given the limited amount of available evidence. The Jesuit Hubert Becher says that Laínez had an inclination to the theoretical, which often led him to set his standards too high in practical matters. Ignatius accused Laínez of acting 'mathematically'. Yet, according to Nadal, Laínez was Ignatius's most intimate friend, the one whom Ignatius probably foresaw as his natural successor. Laínez's complaint to Ribadeneira, quoted above, still talks of Ignatius as a saint; in life and in death, the vast majority of the early companions retained their high esteem of Ignatius.

One other episode presents Ignatius in a less than flattering light. Da Câmara relates an event involving André des Freux, rector of the German College in Rome, the college specifically founded to train seminarians for the very difficult German mission. It is likely that he was a very busy man. One day, Ignatius summoned him when da Câmara was present. Before des Freux's arrival, Ignatius said to da Câmara, 'Do you think, Father Minister, that I do not know how to give a reprimand? Well, now you will see.' As soon as Fr des Freux entered the room, Ignatius changed his expression to one of such severity, as he gave the reprimand, that da Câmara admits 'I was absolutely astonished'.

Other negative judgements about Ignatius stem principally from two of the first companions, Nicolás Bobadilla and Simão Rodrigues, and from Giampietro Carafa, later Pope Paul IV (1555–59). These three men all had something in common: they had serious clashes with Ignatius and what they said was often spoken in the heat of passion.

Nicolás Bobadilla had an excitable nature that caused Ignatius a good deal of trouble.[111] Nevertheless, he always showed great affection for Bobadilla and used to joke about his bumptiousness. During the deliberations of 1539 which led to the foundation of the Jesuits, Ignatius suggested at one stage that a majority of votes would be sufficient when deciding on any one point, since Bobadilla clung tenaciously to his own personal opinions and would not let himself be convinced by anything. All agreed – with the exception of Bobadilla! Bobadilla's abruptness sometimes showed itself in statements about Ignatius, whom he once called 'a rascally sophist' and 'a Basque spoiled by flattery'.[112]

Simâo Rodrigues was another of the early companions who caused Ignatius much heartache.[113] It has to be said that Rodrigues is totally unfair to Ignatius in much of what he says about him. Ignatius demonstrated endless patience with this very difficult man, constantly inviting him to Rome and offering to include him in various decisions about the new order. Rodrigues was determined to have his own way and it's easy to detect a note of pique when he says that Ignatius was ambitious, charging him with using the order for his own personal advantage and that of his family, and suggesting that Ignatius had recalled him from Portugal out of passion and hate, with no care for his good reputation. Rodrigues is reported to have said to da Câmara, 'You must understand that Father Ignatius is a good man and very virtuous; but he is a Basque who, once he has undertaken something ...'. And he continues in that vain.[114]

When Rodrigues accuses Ignatius of using the order for his own personal advantage and that of his family, he is totally mistaken. Rodrigues was thinking primarily of the marriage of Ignatius's niece, Lorenza de Loyola, to Francis Borgia's son, Juan. Ignatius, in fact, knew nothing about this marriage beforehand, and when he heard about it he thoroughly disapproved of it. We know from other sources how Ignatius consistently kept his distance from his own family.

To this day, the Basque people have a reputation among Spaniards as being dictatorial and stiff-necked. In Ignatius's case, it might be better to stress his endless patience. We know how patiently he waited for Francis Xavier to be won over to his cause. On a lighter level, Ignatius is reputed to have waited fourteen hours in the anteroom of a cardinal until the prelate finally agreed to receive him![115]

In his old age, at the invitation of the fourth superior general, Everard Mercurian, Simão Rodrigues, now living in Lisbon in 1577, wrote an account in Latin of his early days with the first companions in Paris and in Italy. Writing to Fr Mercurian, Rodrigues says that he is somewhat distrustful of 'an old man's memory' and does not want to leave out anything of importance.[116] He was now sixty-seven and he died two years later. It is interesting that in these reminiscences, Rodrigues says nothing derogatory about Ignatius. He tells us that 'Ignatius and his companions were convinced that Jesus was the head of their company, that Jesus founded the Society'.[117] Rodrigues also tells us that when in Paris initially 'he had never before had anything to do with Father Ignatius, but only after hearing of his great sanctity he decided to lay open to him all his thoughts and feelings.'[118] Ignatius had clearly created a very positive impression on the young Rodrigues, notwithstanding the human difficulties that may have marred their subsequent relationship.

We have had occasion already to meet Giampietro Carafa in our story of Ignatius. He was one of the founders of the Theatine Order, established in 1524. In Venice in 1536, before Ignatius was ordained, Carafa was greatly insulted to receive a letter from him criticising not only his personal lifestyle, but the conduct of the Theatines as well, and suggesting how they might be more apostolically effective. Carafa took umbrage at such audacity coming, as it did, from a mere layman.

In 1555, the beloved Pope Marcellus II died of a stroke after a reign of only twenty-two days. When the news arrived that Cardinal Carafa had been elected as Pope Paul IV, Ignatius was at recreation with his fellow Jesuits. His facial expression is said to have altered perceptibly, and he quickly retired for a short period of prayer. On his return, however, he appeared outwardly calm, and ever afterwards spoke of the new pope only with praise.[119]

One historian of the papacy said of Pope Paul IV that he was 'often imprudent in his utterances and generally unnecessarily rude and caustic'. It seemed that he knew no guile and no hypocrisy, but indulged 'in the strongest, coarsest language, like a true Southern Italian'.[120] Notwithstanding his first encounter with Ignatius by letter in 1536, Paul always showed himself quite friendly toward Ignatius. He never allowed Ignatius to stay kneeling before him with his head uncovered, as seems to have been the norm in the papal presence in those days. After Ignatius's death, however, Paul seems to have changed in his attitude. He accused Ignatius of becoming superior general in a tyrannical election, and of ruling the society as a tyrant. He also sneered that the order had lost its 'idol' with the passing of Ignatius.[121] Against these criticisms is the fact that Ignatius twice begged not to be chosen as superior general and subsequently, on two occasions, begged to be allowed to resign.

How might we explain Ignatius's apparent inconsistent treatment of his brother Jesuits? I suggest that an answer might be found in the quotation I gave earlier from Pedro de Ribadeneira: 'To those who were infants in the way of virtue, he gave milk; to those who were making progress he gave bread with crusts; and those who had reached a certain degree of advancement he treated with greater rigour so that they would run at full speed towards perfection.' Ignatius knew his men well. He knew from experience that Juan de Polanco, Jerónimo Nadal, Diego Laínez and André des Freux had reached a degree of spiritual advancement. He entrusted them with central offices in the early society. He had total confidence in them. Well before psychology was identified as a science, Ignatius was an astute psychologist, as familiarity with the Spiritual Exercises and his other writings makes clear. Ignatius knew that there were times when it was necessary to give strong encouragement and support, particularly to beginners in the spiritual life and to those who were weak or undergoing temptation. In the case of those making progress, he judged that such overt support should be eased up a little if they were to grow further. Finally, for fear of creating dependency on himself rather than on God, he deemed it appropriate to withdraw external signs of approval from those who were far advanced.

It is worth mentioning that the word 'friendship' occurs rarely in the *Memoriale* On the other hand, the word 'love' appears frequently, usually to describe Ignatius's attitude towards other Jesuits. Da Câmara notes that Ignatius was 'affable towards all, familiar with none'. (109) More telling, perhaps, is another passage from the *Memoriale*: 'Our Father once said – a few days ago – that if anyone measured his affection by the way he showed it externally, that person would be greatly deceived, and the same of his lack of love or in his harsh treatment.' Then, interestingly, Da Câmara echoes Ribadeneira when he says, 'We may say of the Father that ... he gives help to the weak ... in a spirit of gentleness ... and that he gives those already robust dry bread and food for grown men'. (105)

Paul IV's remarks on the extraordinary esteem in which Ignatius was held in the early Society are not too far off the mark. In the canonical process concerning the canonisation of Ignatius, held at Madrid in

1595, Pedro de Ribadeneira testified as follows:

> It is certain that some fathers of the Society when considered as individuals, like Pierre Favre, Diego Laínez, Francis Xavier, Francis Borgia[122] and others, were like dwarfs compared to a giant when they were compared to Ignatius. They recognised this themselves and so stood before him in reverent homage.[123]

Most of those who came close to Ignatius held him in the highest esteem as a man of deep conviction and an inspirational leader. But there were others who were less enthusiastic, for whatever reason, and who did not hesitate to point out his human failings. That he was human should not surprise us. It can prevent us placing him on an unreachable pedestal, and that is surely a good thing. Even the greatest saints have feet of clay, and in acknowledging their weaknesses we are helped to be more optimistic about our own chances for the next life!

PART 2

The Spirituality of St Ignatius Loyola

CHAPTER 15

The Spiritual Exercises

In almost every chapter of this book so far the *Spiritual Exercises* have been mentioned.[124] The story of Ignatius provides a good background to understanding them better. We have seen how Ignatius, during his convalescence in Loyola, began to notice the changes of mood that took place within him as he thought about worldly things and then about spiritual matters. We have noticed how he began making notes for himself when something struck him while reading *The Life of Christ* and *The Lives of the Saints*. Then, as he improved in health, he began to engage in spiritual conversations with others in the castle of Loyola.

Genesis of the Spiritual Exercises
During his sojourn at Manresa, Ignatius not only prayed for long hours; he also kept notes about what he was personally experiencing in prayer and in daily living. Ignatius had the feeling that sharing his own experiences of spiritual matters would 'help souls', an expression he uses frequently when talking about helping other people spiritually. He continued to work on his text of the *Spiritual Exercises* during his years of study, right up to and including his time in Paris.

The Spanish Inquisition questioned Ignatius on several occasions, and even imprisoned him in Alcalá for forty-two days while it examined the content and form of Ignatius's prayer meetings, especially with women.

At Salamanca his own notes of his *Spiritual Exercises* were taken from him by the vicar-general and examined by four theologians for their Catholic orthodoxy. It is hard to think of another saint who has been more often examined by the Inquisition, and yet, in every investigation, Ignatius's writings and teaching were found to be orthodox. The *Spiritual Exercises* were finally and formally approved by Pope Paul III in 1548.

In Paris, Ignatius began to give the Spiritual Exercises to his early companions, notably Pierre Favre and Francis Xavier. On his eventual arrival in Rome after his ordination, the first thing he did was to give the full Spiritual Exercises to Pedro Ortiz at the Benedictine monastery of Monte Cassino. They spent forty days together, a length of time that shows the essential importance Ignatius gave to this work of giving the Exercises. Ortiz afterwards described the experience as 'this tremendous favour from Ignatius'.

A complete study of Ignatius's spirituality has to take full account of *The Autobiography* and the *Spiritual Diary,* both of which have been mentioned already, as well as the *Spiritual Exercises*. Attention should also be paid to the *Constitutions* of the Society of Jesus and to the roughly 7,000 letters and instructions that Ignatius wrote, which are still extant. But since this is not an academic study, and is more directed to 'helping souls' in a pastoral manner, the focus here will be on *the* essential document in Ignatian spirituality, *The Spiritual Exercises*.

Experiencing the Spiritual Exercises

It is necessary to stress at the outset that *The Spiritual Exercises* is not a book to be bought and read as one might read, say, *The Confessions of Saint Augustine* or any secular novel. Before the *Spiritual Exercises* ever became a published text, they were an experience to be undergone. For us, too, the Spiritual Exercises are similarly to be *experienced*, not read. In fact, it is possible to do the Spiritual Exercises without ever having seen the book at all! The book is really a handbook for 'the one who gives the Exercises' to another.[125]

At this stage, it may be helpful to make some initial distinctions. There are different ways for a person to make the Spiritual Exercises.

The classic way is to devote thirty full days of silence in the quiet and seclusion of a retreat centre or some other sheltered place. It has to be admitted that only a very privileged few can afford the time and, indeed, the expense incurred in making the Spiritual Exercises in this way.

During the classic thirty-day silent retreat, it is usual for the retreatant to meet with the director for an agreed length of time each day, in order to review the experience of prayer and reflection, and to talk over how the day has been for the retreatant. Ordinarily, the retreatant will pray for four or five hours every day with the aid of passages of scripture suggested by the director. With so much time spent in prayer and silence a lot can happen interiorly, so there is frequently much to discuss during the daily session with the director.

Another way of experiencing the Spiritual Exercises is sometimes called the Exercises in Daily Life, or the Nineteenth Annotation Exercises. The reference here is to the nineteenth of the twenty introductory annotations Ignatius has placed at the beginning of the *Spiritual Exercises*. In this annotation, Ignatius outlines how it is possible for people who wish to make the full Spiritual Exercises, but are unable to set thirty days aside, to do so. In this case, the retreat is made over a period of nine to twelve months. The retreatant prays for an hour each day, followed by a further period of reflection, and then meets with the director once a week or once a fortnight. This obviously demands a generous commitment of time on the part of the retreatant and the director.

The Spiritual Exercises are divided into four 'weeks', but these 'weeks' are only rough divisions of the thirty days, and do not necessarily consist of seven days each. The first week frequently lasts up to eight days; the second could take up to twelve days; the third and fourth are usually shorter, perhaps four or five days each. The whole retreat should take thirty days, more or less.

Not everyone will be ready to do a thirty-day or a Nineteenth Annotation retreat. Ignatius was adamant that the Exercises should be adapted 'to the dispositions of the person who wishes to receive them' (18), and so some people may opt for some shorter adaptation of the Exercises – maybe a three-day, six-day or eight-day retreat, or even a day of reflection every month. A flexible approach towards the retreatant is of the essence in Ignatius's spirituality.

Purpose of the Spiritual Exercises

Ignatius knew that people might want to do the Spiritual Exercises for a variety of reasons. Some might wish to deepen their prayer life and their relationship with God. Others might come to the Spiritual Exercises wanting to discover God's will for them in their lives. Here the Spiritual Exercises, with God's grace, will help the retreatant to come to freedom in choosing a state in life – marriage, priesthood, religious life or some other vocation or profession. The retreatant desires to come to this important decision and choice before God in the context of solitude and prayer. Put simply, the retreatant wants to discover God's will and desires to respond in freedom to God's call. So, the Spiritual Exercises are both a school of prayer and an instrument for discernment. It is worth pointing out how frequently the word 'desire' comes up in the context of Ignatian spirituality. Ignatius was always looking for people with great God-given desires.

So, what are the Spiritual Exercises? Ignatius himself helps us here by answering this very question in the First Annotation. He tells us:

> By this name of Spiritual Exercises is meant every way of examining one's conscience, of meditating, of contemplating, of praying vocally and mentally, and of performing other spiritual actions, as will be said later. For as strolling, walking and running are bodily exercises, so every way of preparing and disposing the soul to rid itself of all disordered tendencies, and after it is rid, to seek and find the Divine Will as to the management of one's life for the salvation of the soul, is called a Spiritual Exercise.

This definition may seem a little confusing, especially if you are approaching the text for the first time, but the broad definition that Ignatius gives to spiritual exercises is to be welcomed. Look at the varied types of prayer he mentions, and even actions outside prayer, which he describes later on in the text. The parallel he draws between spiritual and physical exercise is very helpful.

What might be less than helpful for the modern reader is the latter part of the definition, 'every way of preparing and disposing the soul ...'. This is very much a sixteenth-century text and needs to be translated into modern language. The late American Jesuit David Fleming helps us here. He restates it this way:

> So, too, what we call Spiritual Exercises are good for increasing openness to the movement of the Spirit, for helping to bring to light the darkness of sinful tendencies within ourselves, and for strengthening and supporting us in the effort to respond ever more faithfully to the will of God.[126]

The Spiritual Exercises are all about a conversion of heart. They are concerned with a conversion of the interior self, so that a person can, by the gift of God's Spirit within, come to an inner freedom. This freedom makes possible a response to God's loving dream for the person in this life and in the promised life to come.

One important point that Ignatius stresses at the outset is that the director should not intrude too much when presenting the material for prayer for each day. It is sufficient to present a short summary. It is essential that the retreatant prays and ponders the material interiorly for, as Ignatius says, 'it is not knowing much, but realising and relishing things interiorly, that contents and satisfies the soul' (2). This statement is key to understanding the Spiritual Exercises. Notice how Ignatius stresses the personal interior experience of the retreatant through reflecting on what has gone on in mind and heart. Ignatius is very fond of the word 'relishing' – *gustar* in Spanish. So, ideally, the prayer experience does not just remain in the head, but involves the whole person, mind and heart. The affective response to the prayer is central, and is the material to be shared with the director. The director's task is to accompany the retreatant on this spiritual journey and perhaps at times to alert the retreatant to possible unhelpful cul-de-sacs along the way.

CHAPTER 16

The First Week

The Spiritual Exercises begin with a prayerful consideration entitled 'The Principle and Foundation'. Here, Ignatius presents us with his God-centred vision of reality.

The Principle and Foundation

Ignatius holds that we, and all of creation, are God-oriented. We might not always or indeed often feel this but, if we are honest with ourselves, St Augustine's saying from *The Confessions* finds a resonance in our deeper selves: 'For yourself you have made us, O Lord, and our hearts are restless until they rest in you.' We know only too well that we have endless desires. We are, as the theologian Karl Rahner famously wrote, 'an unfinished symphony'. Ignatius believed that God has placed this divine restlessness in us and that we will only realise God's loving dream for each of us if we respond freely to his loving invitation to be in relationship with him and to live with him forever in eternity.

Given his God-centred vision of reality, Ignatius would hold that we should use the gifts of creation only in so far as they help us in the pursuit of God's dream for us. Ignatius says that we should try to have a stance of 'indifference' towards many of life's experiences. We need to be careful about the use of language here. 'Indifference' does not mean 'I couldn't care less', but rather a freedom, an openness to whatever might be God's will for us. This seems to be a very tall order, placed as it is at the beginning of the *Spiritual Exercises*. We cannot achieve this freedom, this 'indifference' by ourselves. We need to pray constantly for the desire to have this freedom, so that we can respond to God's loving invitation to us. We all know that we are a mixture of 'yea' and 'nay' in our response to God.

When I have given courses on the Spiritual Exercises I have found that a helpful way to approach the Principle and Foundation is to do this very simple exercise. I ask the participants to go apart from the others and quieten down for a while. Then I invite them to ask the Holy Spirit to direct them in what I'm about to request them to do. I ask them to brainstorm and jot down the things they most desire in life. I encourage them to write down as many things as possible. Then I invite them to look over their list and to choose, say, the three most authentic desires that really express who they are at their best. Then comes the second part of the exercise. I invite them to brainstorm a list of the desires that they think God has for them. They are then asked to choose the three most likely desires. I invite them to compare their most authentic desires with God's desires. Invariably, they are pleasantly surprised to find that their most authentic desires and God's desires for them are very similar, if not the same.[127] Remember that Jesus said, 'I have come that they may have life' (*Jn 10:10*). Jesus does not call us to live a half life, but to live out of our most authentic desires, desires that are Jesus' desires for each of us. How will we respond? This, I believe, is what the Principle and Foundation is really about. We could ponder here those marvellous lines from the Letter to the Ephesians, 'We are God's work of art, created in Christ Jesus to live the good life as from the beginning God had meant us to live it' (*Eph 2:10*).

After some periods of prayer spent in considering the Principle and Foundation, Ignatius may surprise us by asking us to spend the remainder of the First Week reflecting on the reality of sin. On first hearing this, the retreatant might be put off, hesitant, even frightened. This is where the spiritual director can be of great assistance in helping the retreatant through these days in the manner that Ignatius intends.

Entering the Prayer

Before introducing the material for prayer, Ignatius begins by helping us to enter into the prayer. He suggests that we begin by making a preparatory prayer. He will, in fact, ask us to make this same short prayer throughout the rest of the Spiritual Exercises. He tells us 'to ask grace of God our Lord that all my intentions, actions and operations may be directed purely to the service and praise of His Divine Majesty'. We can easily be put off by such terms as 'operations' and 'Divine Majesty' – they are dated, certainly – but they can be easily replaced by 'all that I do' and 'God' or 'Jesus'. In fact, this preparatory prayer is appropriate any time we go to pray. We are asking for the grace to desire that this time of prayer will further God's service and praise. What a selfless request! Doesn't St Augustine write somewhere that 'God has ears only for the heart'?

Another help towards entering into the prayer, and a feature that appears consistently throughout the Spiritual Exercises, is Ignatius's insistence that 'I ask God our Lord for what I want and desire'. This is often referred to in Latin as the *id quod volo* – that which I desire. Notice again Ignatius's emphasis on desire. It would surely be a good thing, before any period of prayer, to ask myself what it is that I desire from this prayer. My desire may simply be to rest in the presence of the Lord or to feel the closeness, compassion or forgiveness of God. My desire will vary according to circumstance, especially, for instance, if my prayer is one of petition for someone who is seriously ill. We should never doubt that the prayer of petition is an excellent form of prayer, especially when made on behalf of others.

In the Spiritual Exercises Ignatius often tells us specifically what grace to pray for from God. The grace desired will vary, of course, depending on the subject matter of my prayer and the stage I am at in the Spiritual Exercises. In the first exercise of the First Week, Ignatius tells me to ask for 'shame and confusion' at my own sinfulness. Again, this may seem off-putting initially. Perhaps it would be helpful to stress that the cause of the shame and confusion is not the awareness of my own sinfulness; rather, it arises from the experience of being a sinner in the presence of a God who is merciful and ever-faithful. We are asking that this experience be deepened so that our often 'rubbed-over hearts', as Karl Rahner says, will be touched profoundly.

It may be helpful here to recall what Pope Francis said in his famous interview with Antonio Spadaro SJ in September 2013. When asked, 'Who is Jorge Mario Bergoglio?' Francis replied, 'I am a sinner whom the Lord has looked upon. I feel like Levi. I trust in the infinite mercy and patience of our Lord Jesus Christ.' That catches something of this grace of shame and confusion.

In the First Week of the Spiritual Exercises, following the Principle and Foundation, Ignatius spells out in some detail three separate exercises, the first of which is itself divided into three distinct parts.

First Exercise (1): The Fall of the Angels

The first sin that Ignatius asks us to reflect upon is that of the angels. Now there is no specific story of the Fall of the Angels in the Bible, only an oblique reference by Jesus when he says, 'I saw Satan fall like lightning from heaven' (*Lk 10:8*). Outside scripture, Milton's epic poem *Paradise Lost* fills out the story for us. These days, some people have difficulty believing in angels, but it was not so in Ignatius's time. Whatever we may think or feel about angels, Ignatius wants us to recall this story, to chew over it and to allow whatever strikes us to move our feelings. Notice again Ignatius's stress on the affections.

What was the sin of the angels and can we resonate with it? In the traditional telling, the fallen angels were those who refused to live in the spirit of the Principle and Foundation. They used their freedom selfishly, wanting to become as God, refusing to admit their total dependence on God. They came, through pride, to the point of thinking they didn't need God. How often have we been there ourselves! Ignatius wants us to apply the reflection to our own experience, not to drag us into a mire of guilt, but rather to bring us to a sense of wonder and gratitude that God has been so compassionate, so forgiving of us.

First Exercise (2): The Fall of Adam and Eve

The second sin we are asked to reflect on is that of Adam and Eve, as found in the Book of Genesis (*Gn 3:1–24*). Few of us would hold today that this event literally happened as described; rather, the writer of Genesis is trying to explain how evil and sinfulness entered our world.

Adam and Eve are not to eat of the tree of knowledge; there is to be some limit to their power. They are after all, like us, only creatures, totally dependent on God. Satan tempts them by saying that if they eat of the tree of knowledge they will be 'like gods, knowing good from evil' (*Gen 3:5*). We know the rest of the story. God comes looking for them in the garden, and asks a question that God asks of us too, 'Where are you?' Adam and Eve are afraid. They hide from God, and they suddenly realise that they are naked. Their gaze has turned inwards. Adam blames Eve for leading him into temptation. There is a rupture in relationship between them. Sin, no matter how personal, always causes a breakdown in relationships, including with oneself. Again, Ignatius asks that we bring this story to memory, discuss it with our understanding and see how it moves our feelings and our will. St Augustine defined the state of sin as being *incurvatus in se* – closed in on oneself – a phrase Martin Luther often used when speaking of sin, which is not surprising given his Augustinian background.

First Exercise (3): The Fall of an Individual

The third sin presented to us is that of someone who 'for one mortal sin is gone to hell'. Now, this too is likely to present us with problems today. Do we really believe that a merciful, compassionate God could condemn someone to hell for one mortal sin? Do we actually believe that anyone is in hell? Remember that, though the Church defines the existence of hell, it has never stated that anyone is there.[128] It is interesting that in his own edition of the Spiritual Exercises, Ignatius writes the word *forse* – meaning 'perhaps' – in the margin when writing of someone going to hell. Is it possible, knowing who God is, to make one single, total, deliberate rejection of the love of God?

We are left in the realm of mystery here. Modern theology tends to stress that hell is the logical consequence of the ultimate adherence to one's own will and a total rejection of the will of God. God risks lovingly in giving us free will. What we do with our free will is ultimately our choice. How have I used my free will? At this point in the Spiritual

Exercises, Ignatius would have us reflect on this question and notice how we are moved.

Conversing with Christ Crucified

Suddenly, the model of prayer changes and we are asked to 'imagine Christ our Lord present and placed on the Cross'. We are invited to engage in a colloquy, or conversation, with him 'as one friend speaks to another'. Ignatius is desirous that there would be a personal and spontaneous quality to this conversation with Christ on the Cross. The Cross of Jesus Christ is the ultimate price of sin, and yet it is the great hope of God's mercy. It is worth recalling here that in the Gospel of John the Cross is the moment of glory.

Ignatius brings a totally personal aspect to this imaginative prayer. He asks us to remember that Christ died 'for my sins' (*Gal 2:20*). Moved by this realisation, I am asked to look at myself and ask, 'What have I done for Christ? What am I doing for Christ? What ought I to do for Christ?' Ignatius then says that I am to dwell on these central questions and note 'what will present itself' to me.

The focus on Christ on the Cross is really the heart of this prayer. Ignatius does not want us to dwell on our sins but to gaze contemplatively at the price of sin. He then wants us to pray before this personification of total love and forgiveness, who paid the ultimate price for love of us. What ought our response to Christ be?

Second Exercise: Our Personal Story

In the Second Exercise of the First Week (55–61), Ignatius asks the retreatant to beg for 'a great and intense sorrow and tears for my sins' (55). We know that Ignatius often speaks of tears in his Spiritual Diary, when he notes his own daily experience of celebrating Mass or being at prayer. Still, the phrasing may seem off-putting to the modern reader, even contrived. Some people may dismiss this mention of tears as a cultural thing, better attuned to a different culture. It is interesting that Pope Francis says, 'The mystery of the Cross can only be understood, a little bit, by kneeling in prayer, but also through tears. There are tears that bring us close to this mystery.' Francis also says that if we let ourselves cry, we can recognise 'the cry of the penitent, the cry of the brother and sister who are looking upon so much human misery'.[129] In the Exercises, following the prayer with Christ on the Cross, sorrow and tears can now be a graced expression of a felt experience of sadness – sadness at our own collaboration in the sinfulness of the world that has placed this loving, compassionate, ever-forgiving Christ upon the Cross. But tears are not of the essence of this prayer. What is central is to ponder this mystery quietly and let it rest with you.

In this Second Exercise, Ignatius asks us to ponder our own personal history of sinfulness. This is something that must be approached with graced honesty on the retreatant's part. The role of the spiritual director can be crucial here. The director must be especially sensitive, and should never show any sign of being shocked, judgemental or harsh in any way for, as Pope Francis would say, 'Who am I to judge?' What is essential here is for the director to be gentle, compassionate and non-judgemental, an encouraging and listening presence.

Ignatius is not looking for a laundry list of my past sins. Rather, he hopes that I would be graced to discover overall impressions or patterns in my sinfulness. As I pray and ponder on my sins these days with the help of suitable scripture passages, I might begin to notice the sin within the sins. Is there a basic disorder around which many of my failures cluster? Are there addictions, tendencies, compulsions, fears, attractions and aversions that subtly prevent me from living out of my more authentic self? Sometimes we can be tempted to panic when we discover these tendencies, but there's no need. We all have them, but they do not define us. Realising – maybe for the first time – that one or more of these tendencies lurk behind our outer mask can be a graced moment of growth in self-knowledge. Such insights lead to growth in personal freedom, the freedom to choose what brings life to myself and others, the freedom that God desires to give to us so that we can respond to his desires for us.

It is noteworthy that during these days of reflection Ignatius suggests we make what he calls a triple colloquy. This is a sure sign that he feels that we need to call on our intercessors in heaven to help us obtain the grace desired. That grace, as Ignatius puts it, is that I may have 'an interior knowledge of my sins … an understanding of the disorder of my actions … a knowledge of the world that, filled with horror, I may put away from me worldly and vain things' (63). The concept of the 'world', as understood here, surely includes the tendency to rationalise sinful characteristics and to defend them against scrutiny. We have seen this tendency all too often in our civil and ecclesial institutions.

In the triple colloquy, we first of all speak to Mary, that she 'may get me grace from her Son', ending with a Hail Mary. We then rest in conversation with Jesus, begging him to obtain the grace we desire from the Father. This section ends with one of Ignatius's favourite prayers, the *Anima Christi*.[130] Finally, we are invited to speak to God the Father, begging him for the same grace and ending with the Our Father.

Third Exercise: Meditation on Hell

The final Exercise of the First Week is a meditation on hell. This, you may feel, is the last straw. Some readers may be old enough to remember the hellfire and brimstone sermons preached by missioners in the middle years of the last century. Such sermons bullied people psychologically into dwelling on the horror of their sins, threatening them with the eternal stench and damnation of hell. While frightening imagery of hell exists in the *Spiritual Exercises*, it must be stated that such well-meaning preachers of former times distorted Ignatius's whole intention in giving this exercise.

The spiritual director must discern sensitively whether or not it would be helpful for the retreatant to be offered this meditation on hell. Certainly, the sixteenth-century language of the text needs to be altered completely to speak at all meaningfully to a twenty-first-century retreatant. In my own experience of giving the Spiritual Exercises to Jesuit novices over seven years, I have always felt that if they had already endured what felt to them like a personal hell in their own lives, I would be slow to present this exercise.

Given the above caveat, the spiritual director could ask the more robust retreatant, 'What might constitute hell in your life?' I remember one novice – who was an extrovert himself – telling me that hell for him would be 'the horrible frustration of being ignored; being in a place of total pointlessness, of having absolutely no relationship with anybody'. For the more introverted, hell could well be depicted as in Jean-Paul Sartre's play *Huit Clos*, where eight people are locked in a room together. At first, they are surprised and ask themselves, 'Is this hell?' But then, the selfishness and arrogance of each one begins to emerge and, before long, they scramble to escape, but there is no escape. Hell could well be reflected in the pictures we see on our televisions every day of cities devastated by war, their inhabitants fleeing in chaos and confusion, only to arrive at barbed wire fences and impenetrable barriers.

What is Ignatius's point in this exercise on hell? That question could well be answered by the fourteenth-century English mystic, Julian of Norwich, in her classic work *Revelations of Divine Love*. Julian says, 'God wills that we see our wretchedness and meekly acknowledge it, but he does not will that we brood on it or that we be too full of wretchedness toward ourselves.'[131] On the contrary, 'Our courteous Lord showed most sweetly and most strongly the endlessness and the unchangeability of his love.'[132] I'm certain that Ignatius and Julian would have been true soul mates in their desire that we feel interiorly the endless mercy of God.

Yes, Ignatius's text does present the traditional horrors of hell, but only so that the retreatant will come to a graced sense of gratitude that God has been all-compassionate and all-forgiving: 'I will consider how God has always had so great pity and mercy on me' (71). These are really the last words of the First Week. And so, this First Week, which has been a reflection on cosmic and personal sin, ends on a note of gratitude. Surely gratitude to God for the past can lead to trust in God for the future. With this graced disposition of trust, the retreatant can now move into the Second Week of the Spiritual Exercises.

CHAPTER 17

The Second Week

In 1974, an international group of Jesuits met in Rome for a General Congregation. General congregations occur if the Jesuits have to elect a new superior general or if the incumbent superior general summons such a gathering to reflect on important issues pertaining to the life and mission of the Society of Jesus. In 1974, the then superior general, Fr Pedro Arrupe, called together a general congregation, the thirty-second in the history of the society.

At that gathering, the assembled Jesuits asked themselves a very basic question: 'What is it to be a Jesuit?' Their response was steeped in the spirituality and insights of the Spiritual Exercises, especially in the movement from the First Week to the Second Week:

> What is it to be a Jesuit? It is to know that one is a sinner, yet called to be a companion of Jesus as Ignatius was: Ignatius, who begged the Blessed Virgin to 'place him with her Son' and who then saw the Father himself ask Jesus, carrying the Cross, to take this pilgrim into his company.[133]

There are echoes in this definition of the experience of Ignatius at the chapel of La Storta just outside Rome (see Chapter 9).

For his ordination as auxiliary bishop of Buenos Aires on 27 June 1992, Pope Francis chose the episcopal motto *Miserando atque eligendo,* which can be loosely translated as 'Having mercy, God called him'.[134] This has the same movement as the definition above of what it means to be a Jesuit: the recognition of my own sinfulness and the realisation of still being called into the company of Jesus with all that this will entail. It is precisely on that call that I now wish to focus.

The Call of the King

Following the completion of the First Week and before entering the Second Week proper, there is a repose day, or a day of rest. Twice during that day, Ignatius asks the retreatant to consider an exercise entitled 'The Kingdom of Christ'. In this exercise, which is presented in the form of a parable, Ignatius notes that it is offered as a help towards contemplation of the life of the Eternal King. Ignatius invites the retreatant to compose a mental representation of 'the synagogues, villages and towns through which Christ our Lord preached' (91). The retreatant is asked, at the very outset, to use the faculty of the imagination in trying to see the places where Jesus engaged in the ministry of the word, proclaiming the Kingdom of God. This is a pattern throughout the Second Week.

The grace that I'm asked to pray for is that 'I may not be deaf to (Christ's) call, but ready and diligent to fulfil his most holy will' (91). What I'm really praying for here is freedom from inner psychological forces – irrational fears, self-centred concerns etc. – that might prevent me hearing Christ's call and responding to it. What specifically this call might be has not yet been revealed.

Ignatius then proceeds to offer the retreatant a parable. Remember that his own background was that of kings, nobles, knights and vassals. Ignatius knew from personal experience that the relationship of the lord and his vassal was one of reciprocal intimacy, friendship, loyalty and shared action. He asks that I imagine 'a human king chosen by God our Lord, whom all Christian princes and men reverence and obey' (92). This king wants to engage in a great enterprise, which will demand total dedication from his followers. But it will not be easy. He warns his potential followers that 'whoever would like to come with me is to be content to eat as I, and also to drink, dress etc. as I: likewise, he is to labour like me in the day and watch in the night etc., that so afterwards he may have part with me in the victory, as he has had in the labours'

(93). Ignatius then asks 'what a good subject ought to answer to a king so liberal and so kind' (94).

At this point, I would ask you to notice the repetition of the phrase 'with me' and the word 'labour'. These words recur intentionally in the text of the Spiritual Exercises.

Let us pause here for a moment. In the twenty-first century, the imagery of kings and crusades has little positive resonance for most people. Indeed, it may well be that we are quite cynical about leaders generally, whether in secular politics or in the Church, although it would be helpful for all of us to look at ourselves before we cast the first stone.

When I used to present this exercise to retreatants some years ago, I would ask them to imagine some charismatic world leader in our contemporary world, someone who had suffered greatly for the cause of justice and whose sheer courage and goodness would entice enthusiastic and generous followers. Invariably, in those days, people mentioned Nelson Mandela as someone who inspired them and whose call they would heed.

Time has moved on. Now I find myself asking maybe simpler questions. They might go something like this:

- What qualities in others have inspired you or aroused your admiration?
- When have you been energised or given purpose by someone's vision for future possibilities?
- What qualities draw you to someone you love?
- What do you seek in a friend?
- What are your dreams for a better world or a better Church?
- Who or what would you die for?

You might like to take some time to ponder some of these questions for yourself. Your answers will be uniquely yours and therein lies their value. I have often been very moved, when directing the Spiritual Exercises or giving courses on them, by the number of times parents have responded to the last question in the list above. Without hesitation, they have answered, 'My children'. I find myself in awe at such spontaneous love and self-sacrifice. These parents will appreciate the feudal parable of Ignatius in their own sacred way.

Ignatius then proceeds to the second part of this exercise, which consists in applying the above parable of the temporal king to Christ our Lord (95). In typical fashion, Ignatius invites me 'to see' Christ our Lord in all his humanity. Christ's call is universal, since before him lies 'all the entire world'. Like the earthly king, Christ too warns that 'whoever would like to come with me is to labour with me, that following me in the pain, he may also follow me in the glory' (95). There will be a cost to this discipleship. Notice, again, the word 'labour' and the phrase 'with me': characteristic expressions of some of Ignatius's deepest aspirations. There will be a cost if I choose to follow Jesus in his mission, but I am not going to be alone in the task.

Ignatius leaves us in no doubt about this cost. He tells us that those who wish to respond to Christ's radical invitation, in offering themselves for the task, may well have to go against their own natural preferences. He then suggests a prayer of self-offering that such a generous person might make.[135] It is important to stress here that some retreatants may not feel ready to make such an offering at this stage. It is sufficient in that case for people simply to notice how they feel interiorly about making such a radical self-offering. Ignatius does not want any hasty, emotionally charged responses. The response will come after the retreatant has spent further time in the company of Jesus.

I have deliberately placed this prayer in an endnote because, in my own experience of giving the Spiritual Exercises, sometimes the retreatant finds the language to be archaic and somewhat off-putting. Many prefer to compose their own prayer of self-offering which, of course, is perfectly valid.

Contemplating the Incarnation

The Second Week proper begins with a contemplation on the Incarnation: how the Second Person of the Blessed Trinity took on human flesh in the person of Jesus Christ. We have already seen that Ignatius had an intense personal devotion to the Trinity. I am now asked to imagine the three Divine Persons looking down upon the earth (102) and seeing so many people losing their way, choosing evil and self-destruction. The Trinity 'in their eternity' determine that the Second Person will take on humanity 'to save the human race'. Ignatius's God is a God who is totally involved in the plight of humanity from all eternity. The saving action of the Trinity is in relation to the sad predicament of the human race. It has become almost a cliché in Ignatian circles to say that Ignatius's God is a 'very busy God'. In their loving and unconditional commitment to the redemption of humankind, in the fullness of time the Trinity 'sent the Angel Gabriel to Our Lady' (102).

It is almost as if I'm asked to view the scene through a camera lens. I begin with a vast vision of the world and all its peoples, and then I'm asked to zoom in specifically on the 'house and rooms of Our Lady in the city of Nazareth, in the Province of Galilee' (103).

The grace that Ignatius asks me to pray for here is especially relevant: 'It will be to ask for interior knowledge of the Lord, who for me has become man, that I may more love and follow him' (104). Notice the progression here, from interior knowledge – meaning felt knowledge, not just head knowledge – to a personal love of Jesus and a commitment to follow him. I don't know whether Ignatius had ever heard of or read some of the prayers of the English bishop, Richard of Chichester (1197–1253), but a prayer of his that has come down to us has a very similar tone and content:

> Thanks be to you, our Lord Jesus Christ, for all the benefits which you have given us, for all the pains and insults which you have borne for us. Most merciful Redeemer, Friend and Brother, may we know you more clearly, love you more dearly, and follow you more nearly, day by day.[136]

You will notice here the same progression that is found in the grace Ignatius suggests we ask for: to know, to love, to follow Jesus. Ignatius also says that this same grace is to be asked for at every prayer period for the remainder of the Second Week. This alone should suggest to us the importance Ignatius attributes to it.

It is really at this point in the Spiritual Exercises that we are introduced to the practice of Ignatian contemplation proper. We are to use our imagination, sometimes with the help of our five senses, to contemplate the various events in the life of Christ and bring them alive.

Here, in the contemplation on the Incarnation, we are invited to gaze on all the peoples upon the face of the earth in all their variety. We are then asked to see the Trinity looking down on the surface of the earth and seeing so many people losing their way. Our attention is then directed to the scene of the Annunciation, where the angel Gabriel is sent to the Virgin Mary. In each point that Ignatius gives in this contemplation, there is a sequence that we are asked to follow: from the vast needy world below, to the compassionate Trinity above, and back to the world below and God's action in the little town of Nazareth. Ignatius asks that we reflect on what strikes us and 'draw some profit' (106, 107, 108) from it.

We are to end this contemplation on the Incarnation with a spontaneous conversation with the Trinity or Jesus or Mary, 'asking according to what I feel in me, the grace to follow and imitate more closely our Lord, so lately incarnate' (109). This last phrase, 'so lately incarnate', is worth noting. Ignatius is suggesting that the Incarnation is not just an event in the past, but is taking place in the 'now' of the contemplation I have just made. The mystery of the Incarnation becomes alive for me now as I ponder it deeply.

Contemplating the Nativity

The second contemplation is on the birth of Jesus. Recalling this great mystery, which we celebrate at Christmas, Ignatius suggests that we think of Mary, heavily pregnant, 'seated on an ass, accompanied by Joseph and a maid, taking an ox, to go to Bethlehem to pay the tribute which Caesar imposed on all the lands' (111). Ignatius's reference to a maid in this passage strikes us as strange. It's as if he cannot get away from his own noble background and experience.

As before, I am invited to enter into the scene, to 'see with the sight of the imagination the road from Nazareth to Bethlehem … likewise the place or cave of the Nativity' (112). Of importance here is the word 'road'. It is a fundamental Ignatian symbol that will recur elsewhere in the Spiritual Exercises. It is a symbol of the exposed, dangerous, itinerant life of Jesus and that of his actual and potential disciples.

As I contemplate the Nativity scene, I am invited to look at what Mary and Joseph and the others are doing and to hear what they are saying. Then I am to 'draw some spiritual profit' (116) from it. For many of us, it is probably relatively easy to imagine this scene since, thanks to St Francis of Assisi, Christmas cribs are familiar to us all from our childhood.[137] It is sometimes touching to see how small children are lost in wonder and awe as they gaze on the manger scene, with their parents explaining the various characters and animals to them. We are now invited to share in that wonder and awe once again.

The third point in the contemplation on the Nativity is especially revealing of what Ignatius wanted to stress:

> The third point is to look and consider what they are doing, as going on a journey and labouring, that the Lord may be born in the greatest poverty; and as an end of so many labours – of hunger, of thirst, of heat and of cold, of injuries and affronts – that he may die on the Cross; and all this for me.

We have the image of the 'journey', which echoes the symbol of the 'road', already mentioned. Then, we have that word 'labour', again with its many connotations of costly discipleship. 'Injuries and affronts' harks back to the prayer Ignatius has already suggested towards the end of the Call of the King (98). For Ignatius, Jesus is born in utter poverty in order that he may die on the Cross. The mystery of the Nativity and the Passion of Jesus is all one. Then Ignatius adds a highly personalised element: 'all this for me' (116). There is much to ponder here. How do I feel about this great mystery? What is it saying to me? What might I do in response to such great love?

Ignatius now introduces the practice of 'repetition' of the two exercises already done. This does not mean that I simply go over what I have already done in the contemplation of the Incarnation and of the Nativity. What Ignatius wants is that I dwell on those parts where I experienced some strong interior movement, whether of attraction or repulsion. Ignatius would have us go back to those places and stay there, in order to discover what the Lord is saying to me through these felt interior responses. Ignatius then suggests a second repetition, which will ideally go deeper into the mystery and evoke a deeper response. Ignatius wants us to lose nothing of the richness and depth of our prayer.

Then, at the close of the day, as a final contemplation, Ignatius suggests another kind of prayer, which is usually called 'the application of the senses'. This can be a very deep experience when, in the stillness of the evening, I allow my five senses to dwell once again on the mysteries that I have contemplated during the day. This is not a time for any deep theological insights, but for gently allowing myself to be as present as I can to the mysteries, relishing them in a simple prayer.

The second day of the Second Week is devoted to contemplations on the Presentation in the Temple and the Flight into Egypt. Again, there will be two repetitions and an application of the senses in the stillness of the late evening.

Both of these contemplations suggest again the poverty into which Jesus was born and the danger involved in fleeing from his own land. Jesus, even as a baby, is enduring the hardships of exile and actual poverty. It is always to the poor and humble Christ that Ignatius wishes to draw our attention.

The third day is spent contemplating the hidden life of the child Jesus who 'was obedient to his parents at Nazareth' (134). I could spend much time in my imagination contemplating the simple life of Mary and Joseph as Jesus grew up. What thoughts, what questions, what anxieties, what quiet joys must Joseph and Mary have experienced? And then there was the terrible anxiety of losing the twelve-year-old Jesus for three days and the joy and relief of discovering him among the doctors in the Temple (*Lk 2:41–50*). Jesus' strange reply to Mary's question on that occasion must have puzzled them: 'Why were you looking for me? Did you not know that I must be busy with my Father's affairs?' How must they have felt? There is much here to imagine, to ponder. Again, two repetitions of these contemplations are suggested, and an application of the senses in the quiet close of the day. The reader will now begin to see a pattern emerging in these days of retreat.

The Two Standards

Suddenly, when it seems that a pattern in the daily routine has been established, Ignatius suggests that the retreatant spend an entire day doing something quite different. This usually happens on the fourth day of the Second Week. It is surely a sign of the importance Ignatius attaches to this meditation on the Two Standards that he suggests that it be made four times during the day.

I mentioned earlier that the Spiritual Exercises can be seen as a school of prayer, but they are also – and very especially – an instrument to help a person discern God's will. At this stage, the discovery of God's will becomes a central concern for the retreatant. This is where the Spiritual Exercises are especially helpful to generous, idealistic young people wishing to discover God's will in their lives.

For Ignatius, there were two main states in life: to live as a lay person, married or single, generously and honestly engaged in worldly affairs, or to live as a priest or religious with vows of poverty, chastity and obedience. As an introduction to what is to come, Ignatius asks that we 'investigate and ask in what life or state his Divine Majesty wants to be served by us' (135). This suggests that there is an element of active search on our part, as well as a listening to the promptings of God in our hearts.

In order that we might not be deceived in our search for God's will, Ignatius asks us to consider how Christ wishes to lead us and how 'the enemy of human nature' (135) typically behaves.

The exercise on the Two Standards that now follows breaks away from the pattern of contemplations that has characterised the Second Week so far, and is presented as a meditation that is to occupy most of the day. The word 'standard' here can be thought of as a military flag, such as those carried by opposing sides on the field of combat. Ignatius tells us that both leaders desire to have all people under their standard: Christ under his standard, and Lucifer – the deceiving angel of light – under his. Jesus is pictured in a field near Jerusalem, while Lucifer is in 'the region of Babylon' (138). Jerusalem, it should be noted, is the place of God's peace, while Babylon is always associated with noise, din and confusion. The same contrast between Jerusalem and Babylon is found in St Augustine's *The City of God*.[138]

Ignatius first describes 'the enemy' in dramatic terms: seated 'in a great chair of fire and smoke, in shape horrible and terrifying' (140). This intensely negative imagery is designed to suggest the darkness, confusion and destruction that Satan causes. In the time of Ignatius, there was unquestioning belief in angels, both good and bad, among whom were the guardian angels of individuals and of towns and cities. So it is not surprising that Ignatius imagines Satan sending out innumerable demons all around the world, 'not omitting any provinces, places, states [of life], nor any persons in particular' (141). There is a cosmic dimension to Satan's malevolent influence. He orders the 'little demons' to cast out 'nets and chains' (142) and to ensnare people. They are to do this, first by tempting them with a greed for riches and then with a passion for honours, eventually leading them to pride. 'From these three steps', Ignatius writes, 'he [Satan] draws on to all the other vices' (142). The desire for riches and honours can easily get out of control as we search for self-identity and security, leading us to dependence on the esteem of others, and eventually into selfish love, self-indulgent desires and all sorts of subtle and not-so-subtle attachments. Pride is the ultimate denial of creaturehood. It is a refusal to give praise and reverence to God. Pride can be a subtle tendency to establish myself as absolute, to displace God with myself. Pride can often be linked to cupidity – the need of material possessions to build up and affirm my self-image, the mask I wear before others. Karl Rahner expresses this idea very powerfully.

> The desire to be somebody leads ultimately to the desire to exist absolutely for self, and to the attempt to assert oneself unconditionally through an existential identification of self with one's possessions and capabilities. It even leads to an absolute self-assertion against God ... There is a mutual relationship between Godlessness and the desire for wealth. Behind the desire to possess lurks a fundamental fear of life that is rooted in unbelief ... This unbelief is not a mere abstraction: it consists in the fact that a person does not want his human existence to be based on God any more. Such a person knows deep down that he is not sufficient for himself and that he cannot persevere alone. Therefore, in the midst of this innerly threatening situation he must attach himself to material things and try to get his self-confidence from them. This simply means that he identifies with them.[139]

In contrast to Satan, Jesus is described in very attractive terms in the meditation on the Two Standards. He is depicted as being in 'that region of Jerusalem, in a lowly place, beautiful and attractive' (143). There is an obvious echo here of the Sermon on the Plain, St Luke's version of the Beatitudes (*Lk 6:17; 20–26*). Jesus is shown sending 'his servants and friends' (146) on mission. In his instruction to them, they are to invite people first 'to the highest spiritual poverty, and – if his Divine Majesty would want and choose them – no less to actual poverty; the second is to insult and contempt; because from these two things humility follows' (146). Notice that Jesus attracts the would-be disciple to exactly the opposite of Satan: poverty as opposed to riches; insults and contempt as opposed to honour; humility as opposed to pride. From these three all the other virtues will follow, according to Ignatius (146).

Again, we here come up against the problem of language that can be off-putting to the twenty-first-century person. For a start, we may wonder what spiritual poverty is. We find an explanation primarily in the gospels. Spiritual poverty means knowing deeply within myself my total need of God. It is a joyful admission that all I have is from God, that all is gift. It is the spirit of Mary's Magnificat where Mary proclaims 'the Almighty has done great things for me, holy is his name' (*Lk 1:49*). In this sense, everyone is invited to spiritual poverty.

What about 'actual poverty'? Clearly, deprivation is not a good thing in itself, as many people who are homeless or unemployed know only too well. It is important to notice, however, that actual poverty is not for everyone. Ignatius makes it clear that actual poverty is only to be chosen conditionally – if it is the will of God for that person. It is likely that Ignatius has primarily in mind here the person who is called to religious life, with its three vows of poverty, chastity and obedience. But, of course, there have always been Christian lay people who have chosen to live a life of great simplicity and actual poverty in imitation of Christ, Ignatius himself as a layman being an outstanding example. Poverty here means the ability to leave things behind and to live with complete abandonment and trust in God.

What about insults and contempt? Maybe the words sound extreme, but the reality may not be that far from our experience. Sadly, within the Ireland of today, I have often heard people, young and old, say how difficult it is to talk to others about their practice of the faith without being sneered at or criticised for their naïve credulity. It can be a lonely world out there for the practising Christian. It has always been the fate of the sincere disciple of Jesus to be jeered and mocked. Jesus endured such treatment and promised us nothing less (*Mt 5:11*).

The word 'humility' can also be troublesome. It sometimes has negative connotations for us today. It is misunderstood when we think it means allowing others to walk over us. This is not what the gospel enjoins or what Ignatius means. The word 'humility' comes from the Latin word *humus*, which means earth. It means being earthed in the reality of who we are as creatures, totally dependent upon God for our life and happiness.

Ignatius suggests that we finish the meditation on the Two Standards with a triple colloquy, which is an indication of the seriousness with which we are to come to this prayer. We are to ask Mary that 'she get me grace from her Son that I may be received under his standard', knowing now what that might entail in terms of poverty, insults and humility. I then turn to Jesus and ask him to obtain this same grace for me from the Father. Finally, I come directly to the Father with this same request. Being received under Christ's standard was central to Ignatius's life and vision, and the meditation on the Two Standards surely reminds us of the vision at La Storta outside Rome, where Ignatius believed that he was being placed alongside Christ under the banner of the Cross.

As always, the language and imagery of St Ignatius can seem remote from today's world and experience. How might I present this consideration in a more accessible way? St John's gospel can be particularly helpful, since it keeps repeating how darkness fights against light, falsehood against truth, death against life. Jesus says that Satan is 'a liar and the father of lies' (*Jn 8:44*). When Ignatius warns us (332) that Lucifer comes as 'an angel of light' he is echoing St Paul's admonition (*2 Cor 1:14*). Satan is deceitful. He frequently does not come openly but in disguise, attracting us under the appearance of good. He likes to encourage us in our good points, and then he uses them for our destruction.

When giving the Spiritual Exercises, I have usually presented the meditation on the Two Standards by asking the retreatants to write a good deal. I ask them to make a list of their personal gifts. I encourage them not to be modest but to brainstorm about their many gifts. What are their strong points? What do they admire in themselves? What are the good things that others see in them?

In asking them to list own their own strengths, I also warn them not to be surprised if they find Lucifer twisting these strengths so that they become disordered in some way. So, I ask them to notice the possible weaknesses associated with the gifts and strengths they have. Some of them can be obvious. Good looks can lead to vanity. Academic ability can bring about arrogance and make people dismissive of the opinions and abilities of others. Our gifts can become tainted.

Many years ago, a Jesuit friend of mine, Fr Michael Drennan, kindly gave me a list of questions he used when directing the Spiritual Exercises. I unashamedly acknowledge my debt to Michael here, and list those questions now. I think that they are extremely helpful and get to the heart of what is intended in the meditation on the Two Standards:

- Are you tempted more by your strengths than by your weaknesses?
- If you were planning your own downfall, how would you bring it about?
- What kinds of choices bother you?
- What are your riches?
- Where do you experience being driven rather than being drawn?
- Where can you be got at? What makes you uncomfortable? When and in what circumstances do you adopt avoidance tactics?

An experienced director of the Spiritual Exercises, the late Fr Paul Kennedy SJ, used to say that the two questions retreatants should ask themselves while considering the Two Standards are 'What am I afraid of?' and 'What am I clinging to?' I'm sure we could all spend a lifetime dealing with those two questions alone!

In my experience, the great value of this time spent on the Two Standards is the retreatants' growth in self-knowledge and their increased capacity for seeing potential pitfalls or areas of self-deceit. This, in turn, will help them in the future to make life decisions with greater self-understanding and inner freedom. Having their own personal written record of the self-discoveries made during the extended periods of silence and prayer will be an invaluable resource to consult later on. The gift of self-knowledge, a gift constantly mentioned by the Christian mystics as indispensable, ideally enables those who have experienced the Spiritual Exercise to respond more generously to whatever God's call may be for them. That, after all, is what the meditation of the Two Standards has as its ultimate aim.

Three Types of Persons

The fourth day of the Second Week is certainly a full day. The retreatant has already spent four sessions with the meditation of the Two Standards, and now, at the close of the same day, Ignatius offers a further meditation, the Three Types of Persons.

Ignatius begins this meditation by offering a little parable. Three people have received a considerable amount of money legitimately. They feel, however, that they should dispose of this small fortune if they really want to have interior peace. Ignatius's language is very revealing here: 'All want to save themselves and find peace in God our Lord, ridding themselves of the weight and hindrance to it which they have in attachment to the thing acquired' (150). The language suggests that this small fortune is potentially a snare that will endanger their inner freedom.

There is a certain solemnity about the way the retreatant is advised to prepare for this meditation: 'It will be here to see myself, how I stand before God our Lord and all his saints, to desire and know what is more pleasing to his Divine Goodness' (151). Notice that desire precedes knowing: I will perceive according to my desires. Notice too, in the emphasis on what is *more* pleasing to God, the presence of the famous Ignatian *magis*.[140] The *magis* is once again present in the grace to be asked for, which is 'to choose what is *more* to the glory of his Divine Majesty and the salvation of my soul' (152). Everything is to be for the *greater* glory of God, a phrase that points to what was to become the future Jesuit motto, *Ad Maiorem Dei Gloriam.*

Ignatius then goes on to introduce the three types he has in mind. People belonging to the first type are typical procrastinators. They put off making any decision at all, and finally die without ever having disposed of the money. Those of the second type are rationalisers. They manipulate the situation, and confine the will of God to the boundaries of their own unfreedom. They subordinate the service of God to their own immediate self-interest. Those belonging to the third type are people who are totally 'indifferent' in the true Ignatian sense. They are interiorly free regarding the disposition of the money according to what God will reveal to them. It is worth noting that the Spanish word *querer* – to desire – occurs six times in Ignatius's description of this third type. They have arrived at this ideal state of spiritual indifference by 'forcing themselves not to want that or any other thing, unless only the desire of being better able to serve God our Lord moves them to take the thing or leave it' (155).

I sometimes suggest an innocent enough modern parable in the hope that the retreatant will appreciate the intention behind this meditation on the Three Types of Persons. Consider someone who has been feeling ill for some time. A person of the first type might say, 'I haven't been feeling too well lately. I've been having frequent stomach pains. I really should go to the doctor. Yes, I'll go tomorrow.' Tomorrow comes, and the response is the same: 'I can't possibly go today. I've got meetings to attend. I'll go tomorrow.' As Shakespeare says, 'Tomorrow and tomorrow and tomorrow, creeps in this petty pace from day to day.' Through constant procrastination, the person ends up never going to the doctor. By endlessly putting off until tomorrow what could be done today nothing gets done, and eventually the end comes. Parallel cases could be, 'I really must stop smoking ...', 'I really should spend more time with the children before they grow up and leave the nest ...', or 'I'll give more time to prayer, starting tomorrow...'

The second type of person might say something like this: 'I haven't been feeling too well lately. I've been having frequent stomach ache. I must go to the doctor.' This person goes to the doctor and is referred to a specialist. The specialist detects a nasty ulcer and advises surgery urgently. The response to this suggestion comes immediately, 'No, please, I'll take any medication you suggest but I won't have an operation.' The specialist counsels against such a solution, but the patient insists: 'After all, it's my life!' Then, for years afterwards, the person suffers from constant stomach pain as the medication becomes less and less effective and eventually, looking back with regret, says, 'If only I had had that operation years ago.'

The third type of person – well, let's not labour the point. Let's stay with the ulcer. The specialist gives his prognosis and this person's reaction is, 'I'll do whatever you advise, medication or operation. I'm totally in your hands. You know best!' And, following the operation, this person's health is restored.

This exercise on the Three Types of Persons is really a reality check, following the meditation on the Two Standards, at the end of the day. It is a test of the honest disposition of my will. Is there something enslaving me? Are there some inordinate attachments that narrow my vision, cloud my perception, make it difficult for me really to want to discern God's will, or have I been granted the grace of indifference to desire only to adhere to God's will?

Further Contemplations

For the remainder of the Second Week of the Spiritual Exercises, we revert to contemplating the life of Jesus, beginning from the time of his departure from Nazareth and his baptism in the River Jordan right up to his entry into Jerusalem on what we now call Palm Sunday. But that doesn't mean that we leave behind the questions and insights arising from the Two Standards and the Three Classes. Rather, it is precisely during these days, as we contemplate the life, choices, dreams and value system of Jesus, that we ask ourselves the questions posed by those two exercises. Ignatius deliberately juxtaposes these exercises with our contemplation of Jesus. Do we really desire to follow Jesus to the end? Are we prepared to pay the cost of discipleship?

The format of these days is consistent. Each day, Ignatius suggests material from the life of Jesus for contemplation, usually just one event. The number of prayer periods is maintained with the usual repetitions and, in the stillness of the evening, the application of the senses on the same event. Since only one event in the life of Jesus is usually suggested for each day, I may find that my prayer is becoming simpler as I enter the scenes and watch Jesus closely. Some reflective questions can help at this stage. With whom do I identify in the scene? Am I present in the scene myself or am I just an uninvolved spectator? Am I attracted to what I see or do I want to run away from it? Ignatius would suggest that I should return to wherever I experience feelings of attraction or repulsion in a particular scene. The Lord may be telling me something through these strong feelings. It is important to remember, all through this week, that the grace that I desire is the same one mentioned in the contemplation on the Incarnation: 'for an interior knowledge of the Lord who became human for me, that I may more love and follow him' (104).

Ignatius offers a choice of events for contemplation from the life of Jesus (273–87) during these days of the Second Week. This is an example of the flexibility that Ignatius encourages. With the advice of the director, I am to choose whatever event will help me most to know, love and follow Jesus more closely. It is worth noticing, however, that Ignatius favours scenes where Jesus is preaching or calling others to join him in his mission. Some miracles are mentioned, but Ignatius's preference is clearly for the retreatant to journey along the way with Jesus as he preaches the message of the Kingdom of God and as he calls others to engage in this mission with him. The question inevitably arises in this context: to what is Jesus calling me?

Three Kinds of Humility

If I am trying to discover to what state of life God is calling me, or to make a major decision of some other kind, the time for this consideration begins with the fifth day of the Second Week, as I contemplate Jesus starting out on his public ministry of preaching and healing. Ignatius calls this choice of the state of life 'the election'. Before entering on the election proper, Ignatius offers a consideration to keep in mind over the coming days. He calls this consideration the Three Kinds of Humility (164), although it might be more helpful today to call it the Three Ways of Loving Response. Ignatius hopes that, by keeping this consideration in the back of my mind while at the same time contemplating the ministry of Jesus, I may discover what it is God wills for me.

Ignatius also reminds me not to forget the three colloquies with Mary, Jesus and God the Father at this time, once again highlighting the importance he attaches to the prayer material of these days (164).

The First Way of Loving Response (165) is sometimes characterised as the way of fidelity. In this state, I would not deliberately cut myself off from God by breaking the commandments gravely or mortally.

The Second Way (166) echoes the indifference of the Principle and Foundation. There is a total readiness to carry out the perceived will of God, even in matters where no obligation obtains. I remain open to whatever signs may be given to me by God. There are deliberate echoes here too of the Two Standards (146) when Ignatius writes that in this state 'I do not want, and feel no obligation to have riches rather than poverty, to want honour rather than dishonour ...' (166).

The Third Way, Ignatius says, 'is most perfect humility' (167). It includes the First and Second Ways, but 'in order to imitate and be more actually like Christ our Lord, I want and choose poverty with Christ rather than riches, contempt with Christ replete with them rather than honours; and to desire to be rated as worthless and a fool for Christ, who first was held as such, rather than wise or prudent in this world' (167). This state is sometimes called 'the way of the heart' or 'the way of the imitation of Christ'. It is distinguished from the Second Way by the strength of my deliberate preference: 'I want and I choose'. The desire to 'be rated as worthless and a fool for Christ' is the attitude of a person deeply in love with Christ who wishes to be identified with him to the point of folly. We might think of two extracts here from St Paul's first letter to the Corinthians: 'Make no mistake about it: if any of you thinks of himself as wise, in the ordinary sense of the word, then he must learn to be a fool before he can be wise', and 'Here we are, fools for Christ's sake ...' (*1 Cor 3:18–20; 1 Cor 4:10*). Notice Ignatius's consistent stress on the poor Christ whom I may be invited to follow.

I cannot achieve any of this response relying only on myself; it is always 'with Christ'. It is 'with Christ' that I am walking the road of discipleship in the remaining days of this Second Week and, as I do so, I ask to hear his call to me personally. Being especially sensitive to the whisperings of Christ is essential if I have come to the Spiritual Exercises to deepen my Christian commitment. It is even more essential if I am asking to know God's will for me in my choice of a future state in life.

The First Time for Making a Decision

Before coming to make a major decision – or 'election', as it is called in the Exercises – Ignatius reminds me of the Principle and Foundation from the very beginning of the retreat: 'In every good election, as far as depends on us, the eye of our intention ought to be simple, only looking at what we are created for, namely the praise of God our Lord and the salvation of our souls. And so, I ought to choose whatever I do, that it may help me for the end for which I am created' (169). I must first keep this end clearly in view, and only then choose the means, whether it be marriage, religious life or priesthood, to be a doctor or a scientist or whatever. The choice I am to make ought to be between states that are good in themselves, states in which it is possible to love and serve God and others. The choice Ignatius has in mind is not between good and evil. I am not praying about being a drug-trafficker!

Ignatius suggests that there are three 'times' – or three occasions - for making a good decision (175). The first time is 'an occasion when God our Lord moves and attracts the will in such a way that a devout person, without doubting or being able to doubt, carries out what is proposed' (175). In this instance, the evidence as regards the choice is decisive and unambiguous and my response is one of simple assent. Ignatius seems to suggest that this first-time experience is rare. He gives the examples of the sudden conversion of St Paul on the road to Damascus or the call of Matthew (*Acts 9:1–19; Mt 9:9; Mk 2:13–14*). Yet, such decisive moments are not unknown. Did you ever have the experience of suddenly feeling yourself called to do something, knowing with absolute certainty that this is what you must do?

The Second Time for Making a Decision

The second time for making a good decision is a process rather than a single event. I experience different spiritual movements within me, drawing me in different ways. I pay attention to attractions and repulsions within, and if the attraction towards a certain choice lasts, then I go that way. It is good to recall here Ignatius's own experience on his sickbed in Loyola, and the lasting peace and attraction he felt after reading about the saints. Ignatius saw this second time as the usual experience of retreatants, 'when enough light and knowledge is received by experience of consolations and desolations, and by the experience of the discernment of various spirits' (176). I will treat specifically of what Ignatius meant by consolation, desolation and discernment of spirits in a later chapter. Have you ever experienced opposite attractions – alternating moments of peace, anxiety, inner turmoil – when trying to come to a life-defining decision? I know that I did when I was trying to decide whether I would become a Jesuit or not.

The Third Time for Making a Decision

The third time for making a good decision is when one experiences a time of quiet (177). There is an absence of felt spiritual movements of consolation or desolation, but there is also a freedom from negative feelings of worry, anger or restlessness. I use my reason to discover God's will for me. I keep my end in view as stated in the Principle and Foundation (23) and then, using my reason, choose what is most conducive to that end. Have you ever had the experience of your reason showing you clearly what to decide in a given situation? I'm sure you have!

Ignatius then goes on to say more about making a decision in this third time. My fundamental disposition, he says, echoing the Principle and Foundation once again, must be 'to keep as aim the end for which I am created'. Uncertain which of two choices to make, I should be 'in the middle, like the pointer of a balance, in order to be ready to follow that which I shall perceive more to the glory and praise of God and the salvation of my soul' (179). I ask God 'to move my will', showing me what I ought to do, while also reasoning about the matter myself. So, I am praying that the Spirit will enlighten my mind and will.

Then Ignatius outlines 'two ways to make a sound and good election' during this third time (178–88). Ignatius is nothing if not practical. In the first way he asks that I list the advantages and disadvantages of two potential choices. I will look over my lists, compare them and see where 'reason more inclines' (182). I will follow the inclination of my reason. This is a very practical method for making a decision and one that I've sometimes used with retreatants, who have found it a very rewarding experience. There is also the practical advantage that retreatants have in their possession afterwards a written record of their own personal reasons for choosing the way they did.

The second way of making 'a good and sound election' in this third time is to employ some imaginative techniques. The first involves role-playing (184). I am to imagine another person and 'consider what I would tell him to do and elect for the greater service of God our Lord, and the greater perfection of his soul' (185). I myself will then choose what I have advised this imaginary person to do.

Ignatius goes further (186). He suggests that I imagine myself 'at the point of death', and ask myself what decision I would wish to have made at that time. I decide according to my response.

In a still further suggestion, Ignatius asks me to imagine that I am at the Day of Judgement (187). What decision would I wish I had made? I decide according to my response.

In each of these instances of making a decision based on reason, Ignatius insists that the decision must be brought in prayer to God for confirmation, so that 'his Divine Majesty may be pleased to receive and confirm it if it is to his greater service and praise' (183). For Ignatius, no real confirmation of a major decision can be gained from cold rationalising alone. There must be an affective response before the final definitive judgement can be made. My final decision should be confirmed by an abiding sense of inner peace.

If an election is to be made during the retreat, I usually come to deal with it in the latter part of the Second Week of the Spiritual Exercises. The contemplations on the life and ministry of Jesus have been ongoing all this time, so I have been trying to decide on a state of life as I walk along the road of discipleship with Jesus as he heads for Jerusalem. Ideally, my election will be confirmed in the Third and Fourth Weeks of the Spiritual Exercises. But the Second Week of the Spiritual Exercises is a long and often psychologically tiring one, and so there is normally a 'day of repose' before entering into the Third Week.

CHAPTER 18

The Third Week

The Third Week of the Spiritual Exercises is sometimes referred to as an extended Way of the Cross, during which I am asked to walk step by step with Jesus. The titles given to the proposed contemplations indicate that Ignatius understood the story of the Passion to form a continual movement from one scene to another, for example, 'From the Supper to the Garden inclusively' (200), or 'From the house of Caiaphas to the house of Pilate' (208).

A Personal Experience

The first contemplation Ignatius outlines is to take place on the first day at midnight, and focuses on how 'Christ Our Lord went from Bethany to Jerusalem to the Last Supper inclusively' (190). The Passion is seen as a journey, beginning with Jesus sending two disciples from Bethany to Jerusalem. I am asked 'to consider the road, whether broad or narrow or level etc.' (192). There are deliberate echoes here of the contemplation on the Nativity (112), where I am asked to 'consider the road from Nazareth to Bethlehem, considering the length and the breadth, and whether the road is through valleys or over hills'. Ignatius wants to remind us that this is all one mystery. The Nativity scene in the First Week already anticipates the Passion in the Third Week. The wood of the manger foreshadows the wood of the Cross. Ignatius sees the birth, ministry, death and resurrection of Jesus as one awesome conspiracy of love within the Trinity on our behalf and on behalf of our world.

The initial grace asked for here is transitional, and is only suggested for this single exercise (193). It is to ask for 'grief, feeling and confusion because for my sins the Lord is going to his Passion'. It almost echoes the grace asked for in the First Week, where I ask for 'shame and confusion' for my sins (48), but now the attention is more on Christ who chooses freely to go to his Passion (195). The Passion is an act of absolute love to the end on Christ's part. I am reminded here of what Julian of Norwich heard Jesus say in her ninth revelation. 'It is a joy, a bliss, an endless delight to me that I ever suffered my Passion for you.'[141]

The grace to be prayed for throughout the rest of the Third Week is the grace Ignatius outlines in the second exercise (203): 'to ask for grief with Christ in grief, anguish with Christ in anguish, tears and interior pain at such great pain which Christ suffered for me'. In contrast to the first grace of the Third Week (193), where Christ is said to be going to his Passion *for my sins*, here Christ is undertaking his suffering *for me*. This shift is probably not accidental, for it corresponds to Ignatius's intention that the Third Week be experienced very personally. There is also a sense of immediacy about what is to be contemplated. Christ is portrayed as being present and as *now* undergoing his Passion.

The personal aspect of the Passion is important during the Third Week contemplations, but it is also important not to privatise the Passion, as if it concerned Jesus and me alone. Christ endures the Passion for all peoples, for our world. The Passion still continues. So long as anyone suffers, Christ identifies with the sufferer, Christ takes up the cause of the sufferer. 'God so loved the world ...' (*Jn 3:16*).

Staying with Jesus in his Passion

Ignatius is in no doubt that staying with Jesus during this contemplation of his Passion may be a difficult experience. He invites us, in words that are strong and may even be scary, 'to commence with great vehemence and to force myself to grieve, be sad and weep, and so labour through the points which follow'. Notice again that phrase 'to labour'. As we have already seen, it is a phrase that occurs three times in the Call of the King (95) and twice in the Contemplation on the Nativity (116). We see again how all of these events in the life of Christ are connected at a deep level, leading to the Cross.

In my own experience of making and giving the Spiritual Exercises, retreatants can be psychologically and emotionally tired on entering the Third Week. This is especially the case when the making of an election has featured strongly in the Second Week, with all the psychic energy it demands. Retreatants, having made their election, may also be on a certain emotional high. Now, suddenly, it seems that they are being asked to go somewhere where they might rather not go.

Retreatants usually enter the Third Week genuinely hoping to stay and pray with Jesus in his Passion. Instead, they frequently find the staying and the praying tough going. Everyone's experience will be different, of course, but some will pray through the Third Week feeling something of the spiritual aridity and God-forsakenness that Jesus himself felt: 'My God, my God, why have you forsaken me?' (*Mk 15:34*). The challenge for all retreatants is simply to stay with Jesus, to be close to him and to his experience; for union with Jesus is the only consolation of the Third Week. The late Swiss theologian Hans Urs von Balthasar has some helpful words here.

> Whether I shed tears or follow the scene dry-eyed with the gaping crowds and the soldiers affects the situation very little. Contemplation of the Passion demands self-abasement, adoration without self-regard, the simple consideration of the scenes, happenings and the inner states of the suffering Christ.[142]

For some, staying with Jesus is not at all easy. The apostles who fled the scene remain prime examples of just how difficult in can be to remain with Jesus through his Passion. I have found that some retreatants – not all – become frustrated with themselves at what seems to be their inability to respond to Jesus' Passion; they may almost berate themselves for having to work so hard to feel anything at all. In fact, these involuntary reactions – feeling somewhat deadened, tired, frustrated or on edge – may well be signs that a retreatant is actually very present to the reality of the Passion, even to Jesus' own experience.

Keeping the Focus on Christ

During this time, encouragement to stay with Jesus is perhaps all that retreatants can be given by the director, and probably all they really need. I've found that reminding retreatants of Jesus' own words to Peter, James and John in the Garden of Gethsemane, 'Stay here while I pray' can be a source of help and encouragement (*Mk 14:33*). As Dermot Mansfield SJ writes in his article 'Praying the Passion', if the retreatant is coming time and time again to prayer, desiring sincerely to be with Christ suffering, helpless about it all, and still giving time despite all the conflicting emotions, then this is surely a true prayer of the Passion.[143] It is God who takes care of the prayer.

For some, the Third Week can be a very quiet time with very subtle movements of mind and heart. The 'much vehemence' (195) that Ignatius speaks of does not necessarily mean that retreatants ought to feel correspondingly intense emotions. In fact, if they are being overwhelmed by their own emotions, the director might well suspect that something is amiss. The focus in the Third Week is to be on Jesus, not on the self. Ignatius makes it clear that in the Third Week retreatants ought to feel sorrow and grief for *Jesus*. Their focus during the actual prayer periods is to be Jesus' suffering, not how they feel themselves.

Later in the text, the exercitant is asked 'to consider how Christ suffers all this for my sins etc.; and what I ought to do and suffer for him' (197). It is worth noting here how the question posed in the First Week (53) – 'What ought I to do for Christ?' – has now become a more focused question – 'What ought I to do and suffer for him?' (197). It is likely that the attitude of the Third Degree of Humility (167) from the close of the Second Week will be resonating in the mind of the retreatant at this stage.

In passing, I would like to draw attention to the important little abbreviation 'etc.' in the passage above. This appears frequently throughout the text of the Exercises and, in its indeterminate way, opens out to whatever may come to the retreatant through the inspiration of the Holy Spirit.

The Christ of the Third Week is very much the Christ of St Paul, especially as portrayed in his letter to the Philippians (*Phil 2:6–11*). This is the self-emptying Christ, seemingly totally abandoned by God the Father. This is the Christ the retreatant is asked to reflect on as well, 'to consider how the divinity hides Itself ... It leaves the most sacred humanity to suffer so very cruelly' (196). As Karl Rahner reminds us, 'We have no right to water down the gospel accounts of Jesus' agony, fear, weakness and God-forsakenness ... The hiddenness of God casts Jesus into a Godless weakness and bodily torment as a result ... The humanity of the Word ... finds itself prostrate before God in solidarity with the sins of the whole world.'[144]

Practical Advice

In typical fashion, Ignatius offers some very practical advice to the re-treatant about how to behave outside the times of prayer during the Third Week. I am, he says, 'to force myself, while I am getting up and dressing, to be sad and grieve over such great grief and such great suffering of Christ our Lord' (206). Notice again that the focus is on Christ, not myself. In the same note, Ignatius advises me to avoid joyful thoughts, 'but rather to draw myself to grief and to pain and anguish, bringing to mind frequently the labours, fatigues and pains of Christ our Lord, which he suffered from the moment when he was born up to the mystery of the Passion in which I find myself at present'. Again, note the use of the key word 'labour', and also Ignatius's stress on the unity of the life, Passion, death and – eventually – the resurrection of Jesus.

While I have written much about the difficulties that some retreatants experience in entering fully into the various scenes of the Passion, it must also be said that others do not experience such difficulties. Some people can remain present to the suffering Jesus in quiet contemplative prayer, empathising with Jesus' pain, isolation, loneliness and feelings of God-forsakenness. Everyone will have a personal experience of the Third Week.

Confirmation of the Election

Though this is not mentioned in the actual text of the Spiritual Exercis-es, it is to be expected that an election made in the Second Week will be confirmed to some degree during the Third and Fourth Weeks and, indeed, in the weeks and months after the Spiritual Exercises. It would be a mistake to make confirmation itself the major goal of the Third Week. While Ignatius does not propose any confirmation exercises for the Third and Fourth Weeks, nevertheless, as a director one can always suggest that retreatants 'wear their election' throughout the Third Week, simply noting how it is with them as they strive to be with Jesus in his Passion.

Joseph P Cassidy SJ, in an article entitled 'Directing the Third Week', tells us something that certainly resonates with my own experience of giving the Spiritual Exercises.[145] Cassidy writes of how directors need to be on the alert for some retreatants 'psyching themselves out of a confirmation of their election' by misinterpreting their responses in the Third Week. Given the radical quality of Jesus' love, a retreatant may be tempted to think that an election, well made during the Second Week, seems foolish, or insignificant or even useless in front of the Cross. In the context of the Third Week, the election may not now appear to be radical at all. Cassidy suggests that, in situations like this, the director can do little else than to continue to draw the retreatant's attention gently back to Jesus. He adds that it might help to point out how the retreatant's focus has subtly shifted away from Jesus and back to self. It could well be a classic case of deception under the guise of good. The temptation might be to think that the election wasn't good enough, that something more radical is being demanded of me and that I should drop the election altogether.

What if the election does not figure much during the Third Week? Does this mean that the election cannot be considered confirmed? Not at all! If a retreatant has authentically experienced quiet consolation during the Third Week, and if no strong desires conflicting with the election emerge, then, I think, the retreatant has been confirmed in the election.

Ignatius suggests that the retreatant should pray five times each day during the Third Week – two contemplations, two repetitions and an application of the senses – 'according as age, disposition and physical condition would help the person who is exercising himself' (205). Later on in the week, however, Ignatius advises a flexible approach on the part of the director. Repetitions are no longer an integral part of the contemplative day, with more value being set on the contemplation of the entire Passion, which is to be completed during the time allotted to this week.

At the end of the Third Week there is what is sometimes called the 'Tomb Day'. This is the final day of the week, when the retreatant might contemplate the entire Passion and burial of Jesus, or 'consider the loneliness of Our Lady, whose grief and fatigue were so great ... or the loneliness of the disciples' (208). Mary has an important role in the Spiritual Exercises. She features in the contemplations of the infancy narrative, of course, but also as our intercessor with her Son in the Triple Colloquies. Mary could be the exercitant's model and companion during the Third Week, someone who stayed quietly with Jesus to the very end, and who felt deeply and personally all that Jesus had suffered. If we are struggling in prayer during the Third Week, it is helpful to remember that Mary is there with us. We could make our own the prayer of the late Cardinal Carlo Maria Martini of Milan:

> Mary, Mother of Jesus and our Mother, we place ourselves with you at the foot of your Son's cross, asking you to help us enter into the mystery of his life and death; to dwell in his heart; to remain at his feet in an attitude of listening and contemplation. Arouse in us, Mary, your sentiments of participation in the suffering of Christ and of the world.
>
> You see how imperfect our words are and how far removed our concepts are from the truth that you live. Help each of us; help everyone who is united with our prayer and our adoration.
>
> Grant us joy in your Son by the Holy Spirit's grace, which we implore from the power of the Father. Amen.[146]

Mary will also feature at the very beginning of the Fourth Week.

CHAPTER 19

The Fourth Week

The actual text of the *Spiritual Exercises* for the Fourth Week is very short – it amounts to only four-and-a-half pages. The list of suggested texts for contemplation of the post-Resurrection appearances is given further on in the text (299–312). The first contemplation of the Fourth Week is 'How Our Lord appeared to Our Lady'. Now, there is no mention of this appearance to Mary in the gospels, but Ignatius, while admitting as much, says that 'although it is not said in scripture … scripture supposes that we have understanding' (299). Ignatius is here suggesting that it would be only right and fitting for Jesus to appear first to his own mother, since she remained the model disciple to the very end.

Rejoicing with Mary

Ignatius was not the first to suggest the possibility of Jesus' having first appeared to Mary. He had read *The Life of Christ* by Ludoph of Saxony when he was on his sickbed in Loyola. Ludolph mentions this apparition of the Risen Jesus to his mother in his book, and also records that St Ignatius of Antioch (c.35–c.107), St Ambrose (c.339–97) and St Anselm of Canterbury (c.1033–1109) all held the same opinion.

It is interesting, if not a little amusing, to notice how Ignatius occasionally finds it difficult to get away from his cultural background. In the scene with Our Lady, I am asked to see 'the place or house of Our

Lady ... likewise the room, the oratory, etc.' There may have been an oratory in the castle of Loyola, but there is unlikely to have been one in Mary's simple Jewish house in Nazareth! We find an echo here of the setting of the Incarnation (103), again showing Ignatius's desire that we see the unity of the mystery of the life, death and resurrection of Christ.

The grace that I'm asked to pray for in this Fourth Week is 'to rejoice and be glad intensely at the great glory and joy of Christ our Lord' (221). In other words, I'm asking to pray for the grace of selfless joy at the joy of the Risen Christ. This grace is in continuity with that asked for in the Third Week, except that now it is joy that is desired rather than sorrow and tears. Realistically, it is not easy to do this total emotional turnaround in twenty-four hours, so I need to be patient with myself and remember that I'm praying for a grace, the gift of this selfless joy.

In a fine article entitled 'The Joy of the Risen Christ', Irish Jesuit Brian O'Leary rightly says that a mother's ability to enter into the joys of her children is the archetype of this experience of selfless joy for another.[147] I remember when I was teaching in our school in Galway, watching the joy on the faces of mothers, especially, at the success of their children in state examinations. Their joy was totally for the other. Brian O'Leary writes, 'Ignatius invites the exercitant to begin the Fourth Week *by contemplating Mary as well as her Son.* Ignatius wants the person to become aware of the nature and quality of Mary's joy, to be with her so that she may draw the exercitant into a like experience. In this scene, Mary models selfless joy for us ... Mary can experience selfless joy precisely because she has experienced selfless compassion.'

An Unobtrusive Joy

Resurrection joy is something very delicate and unobtrusive, hence easily missed or unnoticed. Brian O'Leary correctly remarks that many exercitants are just too exhausted, both physically and psychologically, to be able to receive a grace of profound joy at this point. They are constitutionally incapable of making the radical shift from being broken with Christ broken to rejoicing with Christ in his joy.[148] Ignatius himself seems to suspect that exercitants may be very tired by this stage, since he suggests that 'four Exercises and not five' (227) would be sufficient each day, including the quiet application of the senses. He then offers further advice to the retreatant: 'Immediately on awaking, to put before me the contemplation which I have to make, wanting to arouse feeling and be glad at the great joy and gladness of Christ our Lord … to bring to memory light or temporal things that move to spiritual pleasure, gladness and joy … to use light or temporal comforts as in summer, the coolness; and in winter, the sun or heat' (229). Ignatius is ever practical!

A rather subtle kind of consolation may often be the fruit of the Fourth Week. In his 'Rules for the Discernment of Spirits' Ignatius has a striking description of the effects of the good angel, who 'touches the soul sweetly, lightly and gently, like a drop of water which enters a sponge' (335). The action described is hardly noticeable and rarely heard, like a certain kind of consolation. Remember that we live in a post-resurrection world, and yet the effects of the resurrection are not always obvious. The media tends to bombard us with dramatic images of war and suffering, but rarely do we find stories of those who give of themselves selflessly on behalf of our broken world. So, the effects of the resurrection have to be searched for within our so-called 'ordinary' experiences', in the sacrament of the present moment. How can this joy be recognised? It is often quietly manifested in the slow growth of the fruits of the Spirit in myself or in others: love, joy, peace, patience, kindness, goodness, trustfulness, gentleness and self-control (*Gal 5:22-23*).

Effects of the Risen Christ

The effects of the resurrection on the disciples can be glimpsed in the contemplations of the Risen Jesus that Ignatius suggests. He notes that 'the divinity, which seemed to hide itself in the Passion, now appears and shows itself so marvellously in the holy Resurrection by its true and most holy effects' (223). When we examine the stories of the disciples who experienced these apparitions, we can see that they have a number of elements in common.

- Jesus is the same, but different. He still bears the marks of the wounds on his hands and feet. He sits down to share meals with his disciples. He has a capacity to appear and disappear and even to walk through closed doors.

- Jesus always takes the initiative in these encounters. He meets the disciples exactly as they are, in their pain, distress, doubt or confusion. In meeting them, they are transformed. Think, for example, of Jesus' meeting with Mary Magdalen in the garden; with the two disciples on the road to Emmaus; and of the appearance to the group of disciples who were gathered behind closed doors (*Jn 20:11–18; Lk 24:13–35; Jn 20:19–29*).

- Jesus comes bringing consolation and joy to each of the disciples. The ministry of the Risen Jesus is a ministry of consolation. He consoles by reassuring his friends of his identity in difference.

- The Risen Jesus gives a commission to his disciples. He sends them out in his name to continue preaching the Kingdom of God, the ministry which he himself has begun. We see the courage and the boldness with which the disciples set about this commission in the Acts of the Apostles and the letters of St Paul. Fearless in their preaching the good news of the resurrection, many will pay the ultimate price of martyrdom under the might of the Roman Empire.

When considering the post-resurrection scenes, I sometimes advise people to listen for four words used by the Risen Jesus when speaking to his disciples: 'Peace', 'Look'', 'Listen' and 'Go'. The Risen Jesus comes with the greeting of *Shalom*, a beautiful word that we usually translate as *peace*. I believe that the Hebrew word has a very rich meaning, denoting the fullness of well-being of mind, body and spirit. What a lovely greeting to give to anyone! Jesus does not berate the disciples for their deserting or denying him in his hour of abandonment. Instead, he invites them to *look* at his hands and feet. As he travels along the road to Emmaus with the two disciples he invites them to *listen* as he 'explained to them the passages throughout the scriptures that were about himself' (*Lk 24:27*). And then, there is always the commission to *go*: 'Go, therefore, make disciples of all the nations'; 'Go and find the brothers and tell them ...'; and 'Go out to the whole world; proclaim the Good News to all creation' (*Mt 28:20; Jn 20:17; Mk 16:16*).

During these days of the Fourth Week, the retreatants are asked to contemplate these scenes, knowing that the Spiritual Exercises are now coming to a close. Very soon, they will be leaving the seclusion and silence of the retreat and returning to their ordinary lives. The hope is that they will have been quietly transformed by the experience, and that they will go in the name of the Risen Lord to everyone they meet. Like the first disciples, they are to be ministers of consolation in the world, all to the greater glory of God.

CHAPTER 20

Contemplation to Attain Love

I n what is called the Autograph edition of *The Spiritual Exercises*, that is the edition written in Spanish and used continually by Ignatius himself until 1548, 'The Contemplation to Attain Love' (*La Contemplación Para Alançar Amor*) is not listed under the heading of the Fourth Week. Nowhere are there indications in the actual text about where this exercise is to be used.[149] Be that as it may, it is usual for the retreatant to spend the last day of the retreat on this contemplation, and it is particularly appropriate for this time. But it is, in fact, a contemplation that can be prayed at any time in the days, months and years after the retreat.

Meaning of the Title

I would like to pause for a moment with the title itself. Various versions are suggested in different editions, the most common being 'Contemplation to Attain the Love of God'. Now, there are two meanings of 'the love of God' here. The first is God's love for us, which is absolute and unconditional. We do not have to attain this, because we already have it. The retreatant who has just completed the entire Spiritual Exercises, with the graces prayed for and received throughout, will have experienced a felt knowledge of this love. We are asked to contemplate here the way God loves us, the way God teaches us to love. The model of this love is, of course, the compassionate, all-forgiving, self-emptying love of Jesus. It is the love of the One who died 'for me' on the Cross, and which has been made manifest in the joy, hope and consolation that God gives to us in the Resurrection of Jesus.

The second meaning of the title refers to our love for God, the love that we hope to attain in imitation of his. The Spanish word *alançar* means 'to reach' or 'to catch up with'. Of course, our imitation of the way God loves us will always be imperfect, but at least we can ask ourselves, in typical Ignatian fashion, if we really want our lives to be an imitation of Christ's. Do we even desire to desire to love in God's way, as revealed to us in Jesus?

Introductory Note

Ignatius has a preliminary note to this exercise in which he makes two points: 'First, it is well to remark two things: the first is that love ought to be put more in deeds than in words. The second, love consists in interchange between two parties; that is to say in the lover's giving and communicating to the beloved what he has or out of what he has or can; and so, on the contrary, the beloved to the lover. So that if the one has knowledge, he gives to the one who has not. The same of honours, of riches; and so the one to the other' (230, 231).

In the first point, Ignatius says that action is the defining characteristic of love. His burning desire was to love and serve God and others in all things, and that meant active engagement. In the second point, Ignatius points out that genuine love between two people tends towards a mutual sharing. People who are in love will want to share with each other whatever gifts they have. There is no place in love for selfish hoarding but, on the contrary, there is a spontaneous desire to share all. We can see this clearly in the case of a newly married couple whose love is genuine and who exchange vows of total commitment to each other until death.

Beginning the Contemplation

Ignatius has a rather solemn opening to this contemplation. He invites me to imagine myself standing before God and the whole court of heaven, who are interceding for me at this moment (232).

The grace to be prayed for is worth noting: 'It will be here to ask for interior knowledge of so great good received, in order that being entirely grateful, I may be able to love and serve his divine Majesty' (233). Notice the progression in this prayer, from interior knowledge (not just head knowledge), to gratitude, to love and finally to service. I am asking to grow in loving the way God loves. Ignatius attached immense importance to gratitude in our lives; in one of his letters he says that, in his view, ingratitude is the most abominable of sins.

I am then asked to call to mind all the gifts I have received, including the gifts of creation and redemption in Christ. I am to 'ponder with much feeling' (234) all the gifts I have received from God in my personal history. I am to think of the 'particular gifts' I have received, those special to me. Undoubtedly, if I have just completed the Spiritual Exercises, the graces I have received during the retreat will come readily to mind. Ignatius is at pains here to stress that God is a God who gives. Indeed, God desires to give even more to me, if only I am open and available to receive. I can take so much for granted in my daily living. It is only when I stop 'to ponder' on all the gifts I have received that I can develop an attitude of gratitude, out of which will grow a desire to make a generous response to God's daily gifting of me. Ignatius then suggests that I make a self-offering, using the following words, 'with much feeling':

> Take, Lord, and receive all my liberty, my memory, my understanding, and all my will – all that I have and possess. You, Lord, have given all to me. To you, Lord, I now return it. All is yours. Dispose of it only according to your will. Give me only your love and your grace for this is enough for me (234).

This is the famous prayer of St Ignatius which is always sung at Mass when Jesuits are making their first or final vows. It is an extraordinary prayer, a prayer of radical self-offering, and one that is not to be said lightly. It is a dedication of my personal freedom and everything I am and possess to God and to God's will. Arising out of the experience of the Spiritual Exercises, it is a self-conscious and total offering of the self to God. This, of course, has been the whole objective of the Spiritual Exercises.

When I read this prayer, I invariably think of Pedro Arrupe, who was superior general of the Jesuits from 1965 to 1983 and who spent his whole life in the spirit of that prayer. He was a man with great gifts of intellect, creativity, leadership and personal sanctity, who could speak numerous languages. Suddenly, in 1981, he was struck down with an almost totally debilitating stroke, after which he lived on for another ten years in the Jesuit infirmary in Rome, barely able to communicate with his brother Jesuits. God had taken away his liberty, memory and will, indeed all he possessed. And what an inspiration Fr Arrupe was to the rest of us Jesuits, as he lived on in that enfeebled state! He personified in himself the meaning of that prayer.

Development of Contemplation

Ignatius then asks me to 'look on how God dwells in creatures, in the elements, giving them being, in the plants vegetating, in the animals feeding in them, in people giving them to understand; and so in me, giving me being, animating me, giving me sensation and making me to understand' (235). Ignatius lived in a 'divine milieu' and wants us to do the same. Every creature becomes a reflection and proclamation of the divine grandeur. Everything is a means of encounter and union with God. We might remember the opening lines of Gerard Manley Hopkins's poem 'God's Grandeur': 'The world is charged with the grandeur of God'. As a Jesuit, Hopkins captures exactly the spirit of this contemplation. Remembering this divinely charged milieu in which I live and move and have my being, Ignatius then invites me to say once again, 'Take, Lord, and receive ...'

Next, I am to consider how God 'works and labours for me' in all creation, in the dynamic of the material world. Here, once again, we are reminded that God is, for Ignatius, a God who 'labours'. We have come across this idea many times in the text of the Spiritual Exercises. As we saw in the contemplation of the Incarnation (102), the Trinity itself is intimately involved and concerned with the affairs of the world, and Jesus continually 'labours' on our behalf. Ignatius's God is a busy God. Once again, we are invited to repeat the prayer, 'Take, Lord, and receive ...'

Finally, we are led to see God as the source of all gifts. God bestows gifts abundantly; God is present in all these gifts, God works for us in all of them. And ultimately, they all lead us back to God, because they all 'descend from above... as the rays of light descend from the sun, and as the waters flow from their fountains' (237). With even greater fervour, perhaps, I am moved to say once again the prayer, 'Take, Lord, and receive...'.

A Divine Milieu

To find God in all things, a central concern of Ignatius, means contemplating God, loving God, and serving God in the love and service of others. It is to be contemplative in action.

I trust now that you will see why this contemplation can be made at any time. How aware am I that I am living in a sacramental world, a divine milieu? Ignatius certainly was. We are told that as he looked up to the heavens and saw the stars at night the tears would trickle down his face in awe at the majesty of God's creation.

I conclude this chapter with some lines by the Victorian poet, Elizabeth Barrett Browning:

> Earth's crammed with heaven
> And every common bush ablaze with God.
> But only he who sees takes off his shoes.
> The rest sit around and pluck blackberries.

CHAPTER 21

The Discernment of Spirits

I would like to return for a moment to the time of Ignatius's convalescence at Loyola in 1521. You will remember that Ignatius began
to notice differences in his moods or feelings as he lay on his sickbed. On the one hand, he found pleasure when he fantasised about the
woman of his dreams, for whom he would pursue worldly exploits, but
later he began to feel empty and dry. On the other hand, thoughts of
imitating St Francis or St Dominic brought him a profound and lasting
peace. He suspected that lasting peace and joy might just be a touchstone of truth, whereas a feeling of emptiness and dryness might be an
indication of falsehood. Reflection on this and subsequent experiences
was to be crucial for Ignatius, and was the basis of his teaching on the
discernment of spirits.

An Ancient History
The practice of the discernment of spirits is central to Ignatian
spirituality but Ignatius did not invent the idea. There are echoes of it
even as far back as the Old Testament, when prophets such as Jeremiah
were distinguishing between what might constitute true and false
knowledge.[150] St Paul treats of discernment in his Letter to the Galatians[151]
and in the First Letter to the Corinthians.[152] The First Letter of St John is
quite explicit in treating of the discernment of spirits.[153]

In the Christian tradition, the Greek word *diakresis*, meaning discretion or discernment, has always been highly valued. For example, Pope St Gregory the Great (c.540–604) saw discretion as 'a nose by which we smell good and evil odours'. St Bernard of Clairvaux (1090–1153), the great Cistercian abbot, warned that 'discretion is a very rare bird upon the earth'.

Throughout the Christian tradition the word 'spirit' has been used in various senses. It can mean either a subjective reality within us, such as impulses, tendencies, moods and feelings, or an outside influence for good or evil, such as the compassion shown by another or, in stark contrast, blatant racism. Here I am talking about interior spiritual impulses. These interior spiritual impulses are normally indistinguishable from psychological moods and reactions, but I mean something more than that. For example, when I talk about a feeling of spiritual consolation, I mean an interior experience that brings about an increase in faith, hope and love. Spiritual desolation, on the other hand, has exactly the opposite effect.

The Meaning of Discernment

What is discernment then? It is the art of finding God's will, God's desire for me in the concrete life situations that confront me each day. Discernment is an art. It is learned by doing it and not just by talking about it or by reading books about it. Discernment is the link between prayer and action. The discerning person is a person who prays, someone who has an ongoing relationship with the Lord and is genuinely concerned about God's involvement and desires. The question 'What should I do?' becomes 'What is God's will for me in this concrete situation? What does God want?'

Discernment is the gift of knowing the ways of God and of being able to mirror those ways in my life. It includes the capacity to distinguish in my judgements and choices between what is good and creative and what is evil and destructive. Genuine spiritual discernment enables God's reign to be a concrete, daily reality in my life today.

A key word that Ignatius uses frequently when speaking about discernment is the Spanish word *sentir*. For him, this word carries strong overtones of a felt knowledge, an affective, intuitive knowledge, not just a cerebral knowledge. It is also much more than the fluctuations of superficial emotions. To be gifted by God with this felt knowledge, certain vital things are presupposed. Among the most important are the following:

- that you are a person who actually takes time out to pray;
- that you desire to grow as a Christian;
- that you be open to a God of surprises who is always mysterious and sometimes disturbing. Since you cannot manufacture this openness yourself, you must pray it, since the Holy Spirit alone can give it;
- that you live in union with God and in union with others in the Christian community.

A basic presupposition of all spiritual discernment is charity.

The true discerner must be a praying, loving person, someone who has the gift of what Ignatius often called *discreta caritas*, discerning love.

Spiritual Consolation

How does spiritual discernment work? In *The Spiritual Exercises* Ignatius has much to say about the felt experiences of spiritual consolation and spiritual desolation, because they are the very raw material of the discernment of spirits. We must be clear here about what is meant by these terms. These felt experiences are not to be recognised by the pleasure or pain that they give, but by where they move us. In what direction are they leading us?

Spiritual consolation, for Ignatius, is every increase in faith, hope and love, even in a quiet way. Such energy comes from God and moves outwards towards God and towards our neighbour in love and service. We feel closer to God and others, even at times when we may regret our past failings in love. In the *Spiritual Exercises* Ignatius speaks of Jesus after the Resurrection in his role of consoler. In the post-Resurrection appearances, Jesus always leads his disciples from negative feelings – their preoccupation with fear, grief and guilt – into feelings of peace, joy, courage and a quiet resolution to serve him. Ignatius desired that Jesuits should, above all, be ministers of the Risen Lord's consolation.

Discernment would be wonderfully easy if we could simply assume that spiritual consolation means pleasant feelings or moods and spiritual desolation means unpleasant feelings or moods. Unfortunately, the truth is not so simple. Spiritual consolation can sometimes be painful. For instance, when we confront our own weakness, frailty and sinfulness before God, feelings of shame, sorrow or confusion are likely to be experienced, leading to a desire for reconciliation and healing. These feelings are instances of true spiritual consolation, since they are potentially creative rather than destructive. Ignatius would say that such apparently negative feelings are, in fact, the work of the good spirit.

For Ignatius, the work of the good spirit is often quiet, and ultimately gentle. It is 'like a drop of water which enters into a sponge', as he says in the Spiritual Exercises (335). The secret is to watch where the feelings are leading us.

Spiritual Desolation

Spiritual desolation is, for Ignatius, the work of the evil spirit, whom he calls 'the enemy of our human nature' (327). The evil spirit moves us to focus on ourselves, leading us through darkness and confusion to a felt lack of trust in God and in others. Our gaze is off the Lord and there is no real energy coming to us; we have started to depend totally on ourselves. The evil spirit closes us in on ourselves in a downward spiral.

In the *Spiritual Exercises* Ignatius describes spiritual desolation as a progression, starting with 'gloominess of soul, leading to confusion or turmoil, followed by attraction to what is low and worldly, then disquiet or restlessness, because of disturbances or temptations. This, in turn, gives rise to a lack of hope and love and finally we feel apathetic, lukewarm and sad as if separated from God' (317). Notice here that Ignatius says 'as if separated from God'. He does not believe that we can ever be truly separated from God, for God is always present to us, but in spiritual desolation we feel a rupture in our relationship with God, with others, even with ourselves. Again, the secret is to watch where the feelings are leading us. Unlike the good spirit, which touches the soul 'sweetly, lightly and gently, like a drop of water which enters into a sponge', the evil spirit touches the soul 'sharply and with noise and disquiet, as when the drop of water falls on the stone' (335).

To complicate matters further, some forms of spiritual desolation can be immediately very appealing, for example, lethargy or a desire for immediate self-gratification. Spiritual desolation can speak winningly to our sensuality and to all forms of egotism within us. At such times, self-justification can often play a strong role. We can rationalise until eternity while all the time avoiding the truth. The ultimate effect of spiritual desolation is always to hinder the greater good. It will be corrosive of our relationship with God, with others and with our own selves, bringing about disharmony. It is ultimately destructive. Spiritual desolation is never from God.

Avoiding the Traps

The evil spirit is very subtle. Ignatius tells us that he can assume the appearance 'of an angel of light' (332), suggesting all sorts of holy and pious thoughts to us, then little by little 'drawing the soul into his hidden snares and designs' (332). As someone once said, 'The devil is willing to sing Gregorian chant to accomplish his devious plans.' C. S. Lewis depicts the machinations of the evil spirit really well in *The Screwtape Letters*. In this wonderful piece of satire, the evil spirit is seen using every means imaginable to preserve our complacency and to bring us to pseudo-consolation. He is a master psychologist who will adapt himself to different personalities and characters. He will discourage the devout and make the activist restless. In stark contrast, when spiritual consolation is genuine it always attracts us to follow the pattern of Christ's love, which is the way of the self-giving.

One very practical piece of advice that Ignatius gives in his treatment of the discernment of spirits is never make a change in a time of desolation. Rather, he says, we should 'be firm and constant in the resolutions' we made in a previous time of consolation (318). This is indeed sound pastoral advice. Many times, both in my own life and in directing other people, I have discovered how easily wrong decisions can be made when we are not in a free state to make a good decision. Wrong decisions can arise, for example, from an unfree reaction to a breakdown in a relationship with another person. Ignatius advises patience, with the assurance that spiritual consolation will return (321), and we will be freer again to make wise choices. This is precisely where the spiritual director can be of immense help to the retreatant. The director can act as 'antenna' to pick up signs of potential spiritual consolation or desolation, thereby helping the retreatant to make the best possible decision in freedom and in consonance with God's discerned will for that retreatant.

CHAPTER 22

Group Discernment

The discernment of spirits is not only an individual art; it can also be practised by a group or community. We saw how in Rome in 1539 Ignatius and the early companions came together to discern their future. After Vatican Council II, community discernment became ever more popular with the freeing of structures in religious orders and the involvement of clergy and laity in parish and charitable groups.

Requirements for Group Discernment

To have a discerning group at all, it is obvious that you have to have discerning persons. To be a discerning person you need to be a praying person. Presume nothing! It is very dangerous to speak of communal discernment if the members of the community in question are not, individually, praying and discerning persons. There can be well-founded misgivings about communal discernment. It can easily be a polite and pious name for the tyranny of the individual or of the majority.

To have authentic communal discernment after an Ignatian model, in addition to prayer, several elements are essential. First, there must be a *common vision* of what it means for this group to come together. For members of a parish community, this would be a faith conviction that the Lord has called the group together to be 'church' in a visible way in this time and place. Second, there must be a communication of that vision in an *agreed verbal expression*. This verbal expression in writing can act as a touchstone for communal discernment. Third, there must be *a common commitment to carrying out the decisions* reached through communal discernment.

In addition, *trust* is absolutely essential in group discernment and is never to be presumed. Genuine discernment is inhibited in proportion to the lack of trust within a group. There must also be an *ability to listen* to others with openness, without being swayed by bias and prejudice. It is also vital to be able to recognise and name *group desolation*. Have you ever been at a meeting when there was no energy in the group, with people avoiding eye contact and some talking more than usual to cover up their unease?

Obstacles to Communal Discernment

For individuals or groups there are obstacles to communal discernment, and it is good to be aware of these. Prayer which stays in the head and never engages the feelings can be a major block to discernment. There is sometimes a subtle tendency to identify the desires of the Spirit with one's own personal tendencies. For example, cautious people are inclined to see caution as the hallmark of good discernment; risk-takers expect good discernment to lead to quick decisions. I can do no more here than list some of the other obstacles to communal discernment:

- lack of self-knowledge;
- lack of freedom;
- selfishness;
- crippling images of God, self and others;
- unconscious defense mechanisms;
- bias and prejudice
- cultural, political and ideological blindness;
- biblical fundamentalism.

You can imagine how debilitating and unhelpful these would be to any effort to discern God's will. Two basic questions need to be kept in mind when considering communal discernment. Is there prayerful, genuine, open, respectful listening going on in this group? And is the sharing leading to life or to death? Genuine spiritual discernment always invites us to choose life.[154]

CHAPTER 23

The Examen of Consciousness

To help us be discerning people, Ignatius devised a short prayer exercise, which he called the 'Method for Making the General Examen' (43). Today we call it the examen of consciousness. It is not to be confused with the examination of conscience that is traditional in the Church. Of course, there is a place for the examination of conscience, especially in preparation for the sacrament of reconciliation. In fact, taking time out to examine our conscience prior to the sacrament is a healthy sign of our sincerity and integrity as we prepare to receive the grace of this sacrament. But it is unhelpful to confuse it with the examen of consciousness, as happened for centuries to the detriment of many. Daily or twice-daily examination of conscience could easily induce scrupulosity and unhealthy guilt, and that was certainly not what Ignatius had in mind. Ignatius himself knew only too well the dangerous effects of scruples.

Benefits of the Examen
Ideally, Ignatius wanted Jesuits to spend two periods per day praying the examen of consciousness, usually in the middle and at the end of the day. In fact, Ignatius attached such importance to this practice that he told his fellow Jesuits that even if they were to give up all other forms of prayer, they were never to abandon the examen of consciousness.

The examen of consciousness is not just for Jesuits, of course. Many busy Christians practise it and, in doing so, have discovered how God is actively present to them in their daily routines. The examen helps to deepen our reciprocal relationship with the Lord in the everyday. It brings a felt reality to our spiritual lives. It is prayer that helps us to be discerning people, even contemplatives, in the midst of the daily hassle of our lives. My hope is that, in introducing this prayer, it will help you, the reader, to live a more prayerful and reflective life, after the manner of Ignatius. It may not be possible for you to devote two fifteen-minute periods to the examen each day, but you may be able to stop in the middle or at the end of the day for a short time, maybe ten minutes, to make the examen. Gradually, you will discover its fruits.

The Centrality of Gratitude
When giving courses on Ignatian spirituality to various groups I often ask them what they consider to be the greatest sin of all. You won't be surprised to hear that top of their lists are crimes such as the sexual abuse of children, murder and the carpet-bombing of innocent people. Most people are taken by surprise to hear what Ignatius wrote on 18 March 1542 to Simão Rodrigues:

> Considering in his divine goodness (and ready to defer to better judgement) how, of all imaginable evils and sins, one that merits the loathing of our Creator and Lord and of every creature capable of his divine and everlasting glory is the sin of ingratitude, being as it were the refusal to acknowledge the goods, graces and gifts that we have received, and so the cause, principle and source of every evil and sin; and how, on the other hand, acknowledgement and gratitude for goods and gifts received is so highly loved and esteemed both in heaven and on earth.[155]

These are strong words indeed! Earlier, writing from Paris on19 November 1532 to Isabel Roser, Ignatius says, 'I am confident … that God will not let me fall into the guilt of ingratitude.'[156] And in yet another letter, this time from Venice and dated 18 June 1536, addressed to the Benedictine nun Teresa Rejadell, Ignatius writes, 'For to recall what one has already received is always a help toward even greater things …'[157] These extracts leave us in no doubt about the primary importance Ignatius gave to cultivating an attitude of gratitude for the gifts we receive daily from the Lord.

Structure of the Examen

Ignatius divided the examen of consciousness into five steps. It is striking that the first step is 'to give thanks to God our Lord for the benefits received'. Looking back over my day, I quietly begin to notice those things for which I can be grateful. They can be very simple: maybe the gift of food, of good health, a surprise email or call from a friend, a smile from a work colleague, an expression of appreciation from someone. No matter how stressful my day has been, there is always something for which I can be grateful. Even a difficult encounter with a work colleague may have an element of gift in it, though I may not have felt it at the time. It is possible that this apparently negative experience has something to teach me about myself and about my own unfreedom. Growth in self-knowledge is always a gift. Cultivating a spirit of gratitude and then expressing that gratitude, either in words or in silent prayer, can help me realise that I am a totally dependent creature loved into being by a gracious God. Each day is a new day with an invitation from God to allow him to surprise me.

In the second step of the examen, I ask for the light of the Holy Spirit to see this past day with a generous disposition. I ask help to notice how the Lord has been leading me during the day, opening my eyes to God's presence and activity and coming perhaps to a greater self-knowledge.

In the third step, I review the past day, hour by hour, or maybe place by place, depending on where I have been and what I have been doing. I will review how I have responded to people and events. I will ask myself, where was I called to a more open and generous response, or where did I become closed in on myself, defensive, perhaps licking my wounds? How was my time of prayer, if I spent some time in prayer already during the day? If I was reflecting on a passage of scripture, was God's word asking something of me? Was I responsive?

In the fourth step, I ask for forgiveness for ways I may have failed to respond to God's call to life through my relations with others and through the events of the day. I can also express gratitude for the ways I have been enabled to respond generously to the demands I have met.

In the fifth step, I look forward to tomorrow, asking God for the graces I will need in the time to come, some of which I may be able to foresee and others that I don't anticipate. I pray that my genuine desires for myself and for others may correspond to God's loving dream for me and for others.

An Alternative Approach

All that I have written above has been expressed much more succinctly and poetically by the first Jesuit I ever knew. The late Michael Paul Gallagher, who became a close personal friend and mentor, wrote about the examen of consciousness in his wonderful book *Dive Deeper*.[158] I present some extracts from his insightful presentation of the examen, in the hope that you will stop and reflect on each one and apply it to your own experience, just as Ignatius would have us do.

- Within the small details of each day we shape who we are and undramatic heart-learning can take place.
- My greatest burden is not some intense darkness but the dull irritable self. That is the daily cross of the gospel.
- The everyday is a crucible of our attitudes.
- There is the daily classroom where I embrace the limits of the everyday or else resent them.
- Tedium can be a wisdom experience. There is a quiet daily martyrdom in all our lives.
- There is the daily choosing of attitudes, the constant conflict between yes and no.
- The smallness of each day is the theatre of our transformation.
- I listen to the tone that has dominated in the hours I have just lived, seeking healing of egoism and wisdom for the tasks ahead. The examen is a prayer of gratitude and realism that serves as a quality control for my responses and as a yearning/learning to see the guidance of the Spirit in the everyday.
- By pausing to test the spirit in this way, petty moods can be

recognised and reversed through a glance in the direction of Christ or through a remembering of those who carry heavier burdens. Through a quick 'radar' of my attitudes, the heart's compass can be adjusted and the decisions that make up each day can connect more generously with God's hopes.

- The habit of taking time out for prayerful review of the flow of daily life can be strangely fruitful in overcoming minor addictions of mood or the driven quality that can take over one's disposition.
- The adventure of exodus (from self) happens in the calls of the everyday.
- All is exodus into love and that exodus is life-giving and life-costing.
- The Spirit is the transformation of you so that you can listen to Jesus.
- Grace encounters us within the human.

Each of these points, which well reflect the content and the spirit of the examen of consciousness, deserves attention. Try to pray or reflect on one or more of these points for yourself and 'draw some spiritual profit' from doing so, as Ignatius asks us to do in the *Spiritual Exercises* (106; 107; 108; 115).

It is worth mentioning here that Ignatius would not expect us to go slavishly through each of these five steps every time we pray the examen of consciousness. To do so might be helpful for the beginner at this prayer. With practice, people often find that they are led to concentrate on maybe one or two points. Flexibility in the use of the examen is all-important. It would not be helpful to find yourself looking at your watch very three minutes to see if it is time to go on to the next point! This would clearly be a formula for distraction, drawing you away from the graced insights the Lord has in store.

I would like to conclude the final chapter of this book with a privileged insight into how Pope Francis, himself a Jesuit, experiences his own personal practice of the examen of consciousness. In a question-and-answer session with other Jesuits gathered for the 36th General Congregation of the Society of Jesus, Pope Francis was asked what things give him consolation at the end of each day, and what things take consolation away from him. Here is a brief extract from his response:[159]

> For me, consolation is the best anti-depressant I have ever found! I find it when I stand before the Lord and let him manifest what he has done during the day. When at the end of the day I realise that I have been led, when I realise that despite my resistance, there was a driving force there, like a wave that carried me along, this gives me consolation. It is like feeling, 'He is here'... And when I notice the times when my resistances have won, that makes me feel sorrow and leads me to ask for forgiveness. This is quite common and it does me good. To realise that, as St Ignatius says, one is 'all impediment', to recognise that one has his resistances and that every day he lives them and sometimes he overcomes them and sometimes he does not. This experience keeps one in his place. This helps. This is my personal experience, in the simplest possible terms.[160]

Pope Francis's praying of the examen of consciousness may be an incentive for all of us, to begin it for the first time, or to take it up again, if we have let it slip from our daily practice. Through faithful use of this simple exercise, we will be able, in Ignatius's words, 'to draw spiritual profit'.

BIBLIOGRAPHY

Bergan, Jacqueline S & Schwan, Marie, *Praying with Ignatius of Loyola*, St Mary's Press/Christian Brothers Publications, Winona, Minnesota, 1995.

Barry, William A., *Seek My Face – Prayer as Personal Relationship in Scripture*, Paulist Press, New York, 1984.

Barry, William A., *God and You – Prayer as Personal Relationship*, Paulist Press, New York, 1987.

Barry, William A., *Paying Attention to God – Discernment in Prayer*, Ave Maria Press, Indiana, 1990.

Barry, William A., *Finding God in All Things – A Companion to The Spiritual Exercises of St Ignatius*, Ave Maria Press, Indiana, 1991.

Barry, William A., *God's Passionate Desire and Our Response*, Ave Maria Press, Indiana, 1993.

Barry, William A., *What do I Want in Prayer?*, Paulist Press, New York, 1994.

Barry, William A., *Allowing the Creator to Deal with the Creature – An Approach to The Spiritual Exercises of Ignatius of Loyola*, Paulist Press, New York, 1994.

Barry, William A., *With an Everlasting Love – Developing an Intimate Relationship with God*, Paulist Press, New York, 1999.

Barry, William A. & Doherty, Robert G., *Contemplatives in Action – The Jesuit Way*, Paulist Press, New York, 2002.

Bautista, Ramon, *A Way to the Desert – 101 Questions & Answers on Retreat, Prayer and Discernment the Ignatian Way*, St Paul Publications, London, 2003.

Brackley, Dean, *The Call to Discernment in Troubled Times*, The Crossroad Publishing Company, New York, 2004.

Brodrick, James, *The Origin of the Jesuits*, Loyola University Press, 1940, 1986.

Brodrick, James, *The Progress of the Jesuits*, Loyola University Press, 1940, 1986.

Caraman, Philip, *Ignatius Loyola*, Collins, London, 1990.

Dister, John E., *A New Introduction to the Spiritual Exercises of St Ignatius*, The Liturgical Press, Minnesota, 1993.

Egan, Harvey D., *Ignatius Loyola, the Mystic*, Michael Glazier, Delaware, 1987.

English, John, *Spiritual Freedom*, Loyola University Press, Chicago, 1995.

Fleming, David L., *The Spiritual Exercises of Saint Ignatius – A Literal Translation & A Contemporary Reading*, The Institute of Jesuit Sources, St Louis, 2004.

Fleming, David L., *What is Ignatian Spirituality?* Loyola Press, Chicago, 2008.

Gallagher, Timothy M., *The Discernment of Spirits – An Ignatian Guide to Everyday Living*, The Crossroad Publishing Company, New York, 2005.

Gallagher, Timothy M., *The Examen Prayer*, The Crossroad Publishing Company, New York, 2006.

Gallagher, Timothy M., *Spiritual Consolation – An Ignatian Guide to the Greater Discernment of Spirits,* The Crossroad Publishing Company, New York, 2007.

Gallagher, Timothy M., *Discerning the Will of God – An Ignatian Guide to Christian Decision Making*, The Crossroad Publishing Company, New York, 2009.

Grogan, Brian, *Finding God in All Things*, Messenger Publications, 1996.

Grogan, Brian, *Alone and on Foot – Ignatius of Loyola,* Veritas Publications, Dublin, 2008.

Green, Thomas H., *Weeds Among the Wheat – Discernment: Where Prayer and Action Meet*, Ave Maria Press, Indiana, 2005.

Hughes, Gerard W., *God of Surprises*, Darton, Longman & Todd, London, 1985.

Hughes, Gerard W., *God in All Things*, Hodder & Stoughton, London, 1998.

Kiechle, Stefan, *The Art of Discernment – Making Good Decisions in your World of Choices*, Ave Maria Press, Indiana, 2005.

Lambert, Willi, *The Sevenfold Yes – Affirming the Goodness of our Deepest Desires*, Ave Maria Press, Indiana, 2005.

Lonsdale, David, *Eyes to See, Ears to Hear – An Introduction to Ignatian Spirituality*, Darton, Longman & Todd, London, 2000.

Lonsdale, David, *Listening to the Music of the Spirit – The Art of Discernment*, Ave Maria Press, Indiana, 1992.

Martin, James, *The Jesuit Guide to Almost Everything – A Spirituality for Real Life,* Harper One (An Imprint of Harper Collins Publishers), New York, 2010.

Martini, Carlo M., *Letting God Free Us – Meditations on Ignatian Spiritual Exercises*, St, Paul Publications, Slough, 1992.

Munitiz, Joseph A. & Endean, Philip, *Saint Ignatius of Loyola – Personal Writings*, Penguin Classics, 1996.

Muldoon, Tim, *The Ignatian Workout – Daily Spiritual Exercises for a Healthy Faith*, Loyola Press, Chicago, 2004.

O'Malley, John, *The First Jesuits*, Harvard University Press, Cambridge, Mass, 1993.

O'Malley, John, *The Jesuits – A History from Ignatius to the Present,* Rowman & Littlefield, New York, 2014.

Sheldrake, Philip (ed), *The Way of Ignatius Loyola – Contemporary Approaches to the Spiritual Exercises*, The Institute of Jesuit Sources, St Louis, 1991.

Sheldrake, Philip, *Befriending Our Desires*, Darton, Longman & Todd, London 1994.

Silf, Margaret, *Landmarks – An Ignatian Journey*, Darton, Longman & Todd, London, 1998.

Silf, Margaret, *Taste & See – Adventuring into Prayer*, Darton, Longman & Todd, London, 1999.

Silf, Margaret, *Just call me López – Getting to the Heart of Ignatius Loyola,* Loyola Press, Chicago, 2012.

Tetlow, Joseph A., *Making Choices in Christ – The Foundations of Ignatian Spirituality,* Loyola Press, Chicago, 2008.

Tylenda, Joseph N., *A Pilgrim's Journey – The Autobiography of Ignatius of Loyola*, The Liturgical Press, Minnesota, 1985.

(Endnotes)

1   Iñigo changed his name to Ignatius during his time of studies in Paris. Scholars have advanced various theories as to why he made this change, none of which, in my opinion, is conclusive. For the sake of convenience, I will use the name 'Ignatius' throughout this book.

2   Printed for the first time in Castilian in Saragossa in 1508, *Amadis of Gaul* was soon compulsory reading at court and remained universally popular until its place was taken in the seventeenth century by *Don Quixote*. Every hidalgo was familiar with its details. The work set out the patterns for the perfect knight, loyal, courageous and courteous, the constant lover, considerate of inferiors and at the service of his master. Amadis never lets up on his attachment to his lady love, Oriana. *Amadis* was later condemned by the clergy as an incentive to sins of the flesh.

3   Ignatius reluctantly dictated *The Autobiography* intermittently to a young Portuguese Jesuit, Luís Gonçalves da Câmara, between 1553 and 1555. It is not an autobiography as we understand the term, but is rather an account of Ignatius's spiritual journey between 1521 and 1538. The title *Autobiography* only came into the English-speaking world in 1900. Jerónimo Nadal (1507–80), one of the second-generation Jesuits, called it the *Acta Patris Ignatii* (*The Acts of Father Ignatius*), perhaps echoing the title *The Acts of the Apostles*. The book has also been known as *The Confessions, The Memoirs, The Story* and *The Testament*.

4   *Saint Ignatius of Loyola – Personal Writings*. Translated with introduction and notes by Joseph A. Munitiz and Philip Endean, Penguin Books, p.13. Hereafter, I will refer to this as simply *The Autobiography*. Note that Ignatius mistook his age at the time of his conversion: he was, in fact, thirty years old in 1521.

5   Quoted in Cándido de Dalmases SJ, *Ignatius of Loyola, Founder of the Jesuits – His Life and Work,* The Institute of Jesuit Sources, St Louis, 1985, p.33.

6   For a description of this incident, see *Ignatius of Loyola – The Pilgrim Saint,* by José Tellechea Idígoras. Translated by Cornelius Michael Buckley SJ, Loyola Press, Chicago, 1994, pp.69–70.

7   Ignatius may have been 'a tonsured cleric'. This meant that a part of his hair was cut off on top and left bare. Ignatius's disputed status as a cleric may have entitled him to be judged by Church authorities.

8   Pedro de Ribadeneira, *The Life of Ignatius of Loyola*. Translated by Claude Pavur SJ, The Institute of Jesuit Sources, St Louis, 2014. Ribadeneira was the last of the early Jesuits to die. He died in September 1611, thirty-five years after the death of Ignatius. Ribadeneira composed his biography of Ignatius between 1567 and 1569. The definitive Latin edition appeared in 1586.

9   The letter is dated 20 December 1518.

10 In 1512, King Ferdinand of Aragon usurped the title of King of Navarre. In 1517, Henri d'Albret was proclaimed King of Navarre, his hereditary kingdom. King Charles V of Spain, Ferdinand's grandson, also claimed the kingdom of Navarre. Henri enjoyed the protection of King Francis I of France. In 1521, an effort was made to establish Henri as de facto sovereign in Pamplona. This is why the battle took place.

11 *The Autobiography*, p.13.

12 Ignatius would have read the 1511 edition of the *Lives of the Saints*, for St Honofrio – a saint he came to revere – is not found in the two earlier Castilian editions.

13 *The Autobiography*, pp.14–15

14 *The Autobiography*, p.16

15 Joan Segarra Pijuan SJ, *Manresa and Saint Ignatius of Loyola,* Ajuntament de Manresa, 1992, p.19.

16 *The Autobiography*, p.21.

17 *The Autobiography*, p.25.

18 *The Autobiography,* p.25.

19 *The Autobiography*, p.27.

20 Quoted in Joan Segarra Pijuan SJ, p.113.

21 Quoted in Joan Segarra Pijuan SJ, p.115.

22 Joan Segarra Pijuan SJ, p.21.

23 Quoted in Joan Segarra Pijuan SJ, p.128.
24 Ribadeneira, *The Life of Ignatius of Loyola*, p.39, Number 60.
25 David Fleming SJ, *The Spiritual Exercises of Saint Ignatius – A Literal Translation and a Contemporary Reading,* The Institute of Jesuit Sources, St Louis, 1978 (332). From now on, quotations from *The Spiritual Exercises* will be numbered between brackets. The numbers refer to the paragraphs in the text.
26 Quoted in José Ignacio Tellechea Idígoras, *Ignatius of Loyola – The Pilgrim Saint*, p.233.
27 Humanism was essentially a cultural programme, which appealed to classical antiquity as a model of eloquence. The important thing was to return *ad fontes* (back to the sources). This Latin slogan set out the vision of returning to the wellspring and source of modern western culture in the ancient world, allowing its ideas and values to refresh and renew that culture. The classical period was to be both a source and a norm for the Renaissance.
28 The *alumbrados* (illuminated ones) was a term used loosely to describe the practitioners of a mystical form of Christianity in Spain during the fifteenth and sixteenth centuries. They were firmly dealt with by the Spanish Inquisition. At their most extreme, the *alumbrados* held that the human soul can reach such a degree of perfection that even in this life it can contemplate the essence of God and comprehend the mystery of the Trinity. All external worship, they declared, is superfluous, and the reception of the sacraments useless. Sin is impossible in this state of complete union with God, and persons in this state of impeccability could indulge their sexual desires and commit other sinful acts freely without staining their souls.
29 The Spanish Inquisition, a tribunal established in 1478 by King Ferdinand and Queen Isabella to safeguard orthodox Christianity, was, unlike the Roman Inquisition, entirely operated by the Spanish crown. The popes, who controlled only the nomination of its head, regarded it as a usurpation of their authority and were never reconciled to it.
30 *The Autobiography*, p.40. Dominic Soto (1494–1560), Dominican theologian; St Albert the Great, (1200–80), Dominican theologian; Peter Lombard (c.1100–60), theologian at Paris.
31 See reference in *Ignatius of Loyola – The Pilgrim Saint*, pp.265–267.
32 *The Imitation of Christ* was a popular work in Spain, where it was printed at least five times between 1505 and 1520. Ignatius attributed *The Imitation of Christ* to Jean Gerson (1363–1429), Chancellor of the University of Paris. The work was attributed to various authors at the time. Finally, Thomas à Kempis was considered by the majority of scholars to be the authentic author.
33 Alfonso de Fonseca held the Primatial See of Toledo from 1523 until his death in 1534. He was a generous patron of learning and a friend of Erasmus and the Spanish Erasmians, including the Alcalà printer, Miguel de Eguia. Ignatius had found him in Valladolid where de Fonseca had gone for the baptism of the newborn son of Charles V, the future Philip II.
34 San Esteban was a famous Dominican priory in Salamanca. Among its members were some of the University of Salamanca's greatest professors, including Francisco de Vitoria (1480–1546). Having recently returned from Paris, de Vitoria occupied the first chair of theology at Salamanca from 1526.
35 *The Autobiography*, p.46.
36 See Ribadeneira, *The Life*, pp.69–70, Numbers 98–9.
37 See reference in *Ignatius of Loyola – The Pilgrim Saint,* pp.287–8.
38 John Calvin (1509–64), French reformer and theologian.
39 *The Autobiography,* p.50.
40 Pedro de Paralta, Juan de Castro and Amador de Elduayen.
41 Ribadeneira, *The Life*, p.70, Number 99.
42 Pierre Favre came to Paris in 1525. He received his bachelor's degree in 1529 and his licentiate in 1530. Francis Xavier began his studies in 1526 and received his bachelor's and licentiate degrees at the same time as Favre.
43 *The Spiritual Writings of Pierre Favre – The Memoriale and Selected Letters and Instructions*, the Institute of Jesuit Sources, St Louis, 1996, p.65.
44 Ignatius received a licence in arts on 13 March 1533. Although he referred to this licentiate as *Magisterium*, he formally received the title of Master of Arts on 14 March 1535 under the university rectorship of Florence Jacquart.

45 A retreat usually lasting thirty days where one meets with one's spiritual director once a day.
46 Ribadeneira, *The Life,* p.79, Number 112.
47 Ribadeneira, *The Life,* p.79, Number 112.
48 Giam Pietro Caraffa (1476–1559) was Bishop of Chiete (Theate) from 1504 to 1524. In 1520, he sat on a commission at Rome appointed to deal with the affair of Martin Luther. In 1524, he resigned his bishopric in order to found, along with St Cajetan, the Theatine Order. In 1536, he became Archbishop of Naples and was created cardinal. Finally, in 1555, he was elected pope.
49 Diego de Hoces died in Padua in 1538, the first of the group of companions who would form the Society of Jesus to do so.
50 Reserved sins were those that could be absolved only by a bishop or by certain clerics given the faculty to do so.
51 *The Autobiography*, p.59.
52 *The Spiritual Exercises* (147).
53 Quoted in Hugo Rahner, *The Vision of St Ignatius in the Chapel of La Storta*, Rome, 1975, pp.36–7.
54 Reference to this in Ribadeneira, *The Life,* p.98, Number 141.
55 *The Autobiography*, p.60.
56 Ribadeneira, *The Life,* p.98, Number 140.
57 Ribadeneira, *The Life,* p.98, Number 140.
58 Ribadaneira, ibid., p.100, Number 143.
59 In this letter to Isabel Roser, Ignatius also refers to some of the activities he and his companions undertook when they first came to Rome – opening a centre for the religious instruction of Jewish converts, founding a house of refuge for former prostitutes and establishing an orphanage.
60 Paul III had been at Nice earlier in 1538 presiding at peace negotiations between Charles V and Francis I. Ignatius saw him at his residence at Frascati outside Rome.
61 *Ignatius of Loyola – Letters and Instructions*, edited by Martin E. Palmer SJ, John W. Padberg SJ, John McCarthy SJ, The Institute of Jesuit Sources, St Louis, 2006, pp.35–9.
62 The Confraternity of Grace enrolled more than 100 prominent Roman men and women.
63 Ribadeneira, *The Life,* p.156, Number 220.
64 Ribadeneira, ibid., p.157, Number 221.
65 Philip Neri was canonised on the same day as Ignatius, 12 March 1622.
66 Quoted in John O'Malley, *The First Jesuits,* Harvard University Press, Cambridge, Massachusetts, 1993, p.35.
67 Quoted in Ribadeneira (165). 'The finger of God is here' (after *Ex 8:19*) is the form found in the Spanish edition of Ribadeniera's *Life of Ignatius*, p.115, Number 165.
68 Ribadeneira, *The Life.* p.152, Number 212.
69 See John O'Malley, *The First Jesuits*, p.190.
70 Margarita of Austria (1522–86) was the illegitimate daughter of the Emperor Charles V. She was the wife of Ottavio Farnese, Duke of Parma.
71 *The Constitutions of the Society of Jesus and their Complementary Norms,* The Institute of Jesuit Sources, St Louis [67].
72 Quoted from José Ignacio Tellecha Idigoras, *Ignatius of Loyola – The Pilgrim Saint*, p.466.
73 ibid., p.465.
74 ibid., p.465.
75 ibid., pp.468–9.
76 *Ignatius of Loyola – Letters & Instructions,* The Institute of Jesuit Sources, St Louis, 2006, p.35.
77 Letter, Rome, early September 1541, to Alfonso Salmerón and Paschase Broët, in *Ignatius of Loyola – Letters and Instructions*, p.64.
78 Quoted in *Ignatius of Loyola – The Pilgrim Saint,* p.487.
79 Quoted in *Ignatius of Loyola – The Pilgrim Saint,* p.488.
80 *Year by Year with the Early Jesuits – Selections from the Chronicon of Juan de Polanco*, translated and annotated by John Patrick Donnelly SJ. The Institute of Jesuit Sources, St Louis, 2004, p.4.

81 Francis Borgia (1510–72) succeeded to his title in 1543. King Charles V of Spain appointed him Viceroy of Catalonia, but on the death of his wife, Leonora de Castro, in 1546, Francis secretly joined the Jesuits and in 1551 was ordained priest and disposed of his estates. He was responsible for the establishment of many schools and colleges, and helped especially with the foundation of the Roman College. On the death of Diego Laínez in 1565, Francis was elected the third superior general of the Society of Jesus. He died in 1572.

82 See Chapter 6 of John O'Malley's *The First Jesuits* for some facts about the schools.

83 *Ignatius of Loyola – Letters and Instructions,* pp.329–30.

84 Ribadeneira, *The Life of Ignatius of Loyola,* p.280, Number 389.

85 Jean Codure (1508–41) was born in Provence, France, and received his licentiate and master's degrees from the University of Paris. Codure was a favourite of Pope Paul III, who named him as confessor to Margaret of Austria. Codure acted as the first secretary of the Society, and worked with Ignatius on an early draft of the Jesuit Constitutions. He was the first of the early companions to die, in 1541.

86 Juan Alfonso de Polanco (1517–76) was born in Burgos in Spain. He entered the Society in 1541, and from 1547 was secretary to Ignatius and became his right-hand man until Ignatius's death in 1556. Polanco continued as secretary to two successive generals, Diego Laínez and Francis Borgia, and was himself a key figure in the early history of the Society. He died in 1576.

87 The 'noviceship' is the first two years of the young Jesuit's training.

88 'Scholastics' is the term used for young Jesuits who are in study after the noviceship and prior to their final vows, which follow ordination.

89 Numbers 287, 553 and 816 of *The Constitutions of the Society of Jesus.* Translated, with an Introduction and a Commentary by George E. Ganss SJ, The Institute of Jesuit Sources, St Louis, 1970.

90 Number 547 in *The Constitutions*.

91 Endnote 1, pp.245–6 in *The Constitutions*.

92 Born on the island of Majorca in 1507, Nadal first met Ignatius in Paris in 1536 and reacted against him. Only in 1545 did he undergo a change of heart and enter the Society. He became a key player in its expansion. He was rector of the first college in Messina, and was official promulgator of the new Constitutions all over Europe. He became vicar general of the Society when Ignatius was seriously ill, and was the holder of important posts after Ignatius's death.

93 At the end of a two-year probationary period called 'noviceship', Jesuit novices pronounce simple, perpetual vows of poverty, chastity and obedience and promise to enter the Society fully in the future. Those intending to study for the priesthood are called 'scholastics'. A scholastic may be released from these simple vows for personal reasons or at the discretion of those entrusted with his formation. Princess Juana did not pronounce final, solemn vows.

94 Quoted in Lisa Fullam, 'Juana SJ: Status of Women in the Society', in *Studies in the Spirituality of Jesuits*, 31/5 November 1999, p.28.

95 *Inigo: Discernment Log-Book – The Spiritual Diary of Saint Ignatius Loyola.* Edited and translated by Joseph A. Munitiz SJ, Inigo Enterprises, London, 1987, p.47.

96 *Ignatius of Loyola – Letters and Instructions,* pp.154–5.

97 *Ignatius of Loyola – Letter and Instructions,* pp.294–5.

98 Quoted in Ribadeneira, *The Life of Ignatius Loyola*, p.327, Number 477.

99 Quoted in José Ignacio Telllechea Idígoras, *Ignatius of Loyola – The Pilgrim Saint,* p.606.

100 Fr Cristóbal de Madrid was a friend and advisor to Ignatius before entering the Society of Jesus in 1555; he was, even while a novice, given charge of certain works and indeed appointed, along with Fr Nadal, to take charge of the Society when Ignatius became gravely ill in 1556. Fr de Madrid went on to become Assistant to the second superior-general (Fr Laínez) and superior of the Roman residence. He died in 1573.

101 Quoted from Cándido de Dalmases SJ, *Ignatius of Loyola – Founder of the Jesuits*, p.289.

102 Ribadeneira, *Life of Ignatius of Loyola,* p.338, Number 496.

103 Alsonso Sánchez Coello (1531–88) was a famous Portuguese portraitist of the Spanish Renaissance.

104 ibid., p.330, Number 483.

105 See 'Ignatius as Seen by his Contemporaries', by Hubert Becher in *Ignatius of Loyola – His Personality and Spiritual Heritage (1556–1956),* Institute of Jesuit Sources, St Louis, 1977, p.89.

106 *Ignatius of Loyola – His Personality and Spiritual Heritage (1556–1956),* The Institute of Jesuit Sources, St Louis, 1977, p.77.

107 Luís Gonçalves da Câmara was born in Portugal c.1519. He studied in Paris and in Coimbra in Portugal. He joined the Society of Jesus in 1545. After pastoral work in Portugal and North Africa and a spell at the royal court, he left for Rome in 1553 where he lived with Ignatius for two years, during which time he composed his famous *Memoriale.* He left Rome in 1555 and returned to Portugal. He was tutor to the boy-king Sebastian I. Eventually he was able to retire from the court and lived at the Jesuit college at Evora. He died on 15 March 1575.

108 *Remembering Iñigo – Glimpse of the Life of Saint Ignatius of Loyola – The Memoriale of Luís Gonçalves da Câmara.* Translated with Introduction, notes and indices by Alexander Eaglestone and Joseph A. Munitiz SJ, Gracewing, Leominster, 2004.

109 Quoted in *Ignatius of Loyola – His Personality and Spiritual Heritage 1556–1956,* p.87.

110 ibid., p.87.

111 Nicolás Alonso Bobadilla was born in the village of Bobadilla del Camino in the diocese of Palencia in Old Castile, Spain. He studied rhetoric and logic at Valladolid, then philosophy at Alcalà and theology at Valladolid. He came to Paris to study Latin, Greek and Hebrew and there met Ignatius and the other first companions. He took vows with them at Montmartre in 1534 and was ordained in Venice in 1537. Bobadilla was something of an eccentric and a hypochondriac, yet was used by Pope Paul III in missions all over Europe. Later, Paul III was about to send Bobadilla and Rodrigues to India, but Bobadilla became ill and Francis Xavier went in his place. Bobadilla was always the odd man out. He preferred working alone. He was upset by what he saw as the over-regularisation of the Society under Ignatius. He provoked a crisis between Paul IV and the Society following the death of Ignatius. He contended that the first companions were all co-founders. This was, in fact, true, but it put Jerónimo Nadal into a rage against Bobadilla and placed the latter under somewhat of a cloud in the history of the Society. Bobadilla was the last of the first companions to die, on 23 September 1590, at the age of 81.

112 Quoted in *Ignatius of Loyola – His Personality and Spiritual Heritage 1556–1956,* p.84.

113 Simâo Rodrigues de Azevedo was born in the north of Portugal in 1509. He was of noble lineage. He was raised in Lisbon under the tutelage of the dean of the royal chapel. He came to study in Paris in June 1526, having received one of the scholarships offered by King John III of Portugal. He joined the other first companions in Paris in 1533 and pronounced vows with them at Montmartre in 1534. He was ordained in Venice in 1537. Originally, it had been intended that he would go to the Far East but circumstances dictated his remaining in Portugal. Ignatius appointed him as the first provincial of Portugal. He had a laissez-faire style of government as provincial. He was flexible with formation and with permissions and, understandably, was therefore popular with certain members of the province. Ignatius decided to remove him from Portugal and appointed him instead as provincial of Castile, but Rodrigues did not want to go. Ignatius had to order him under his vow of obedience to go to Castile. Rodrigues was very unhappy with this situation. Subsequently, he retired to a hermitage in Northern Italy. Around 1573, he returned to Portugal with the permission of Father General Mercurian. As an old man in 1577, at the invitation of Mercurian, he wrote an account of his early days in Paris and Rome. He died in Lisbon on 15 July 1579.

114 Quoted in *Ignatius of Loyola – His Personality and Spiritual Heritage 1556–1956,* p.84.

115 ibid., p.86.

116 *A Brief and Exact Account – The Recollections of Simâo Rodrigues on the Origin and Progress of the Society of Jesus.* With Translation, Introduction and Commentary by Joseph F. Conwell SJ. The Institute of Jesuit Sources, St Louis, p.1.

117 ibid., p.1.

118 ibid., p.8.

119 See *Ignatius of Loyola – His Personality & Spiritual Heritage 1556–1956,* p.85.

120 Ludwig von Pastor, *History of the Popes* (40 vols, 1891–1953), XIV, 69–70. Quoted in *Igna-*

tius of Loyola – His Personality & Spiritual Heritage 1556–1956, p.85.

121 *Ignatius of Loyola – His Personality & Spiritual Heritage 1556–1956,* p.85.

122 Pierre Favre, Francis Xavier and Francis Borgia are now canonised saints.

123 ibid., p.95.

124 In references to the Spiritual Exercises, the normal convention for numbering the text is used.

125 It is to be noted that Ignatius never uses the term 'spiritual director' but always 'the one who gives the Exercises'. For Ignatius, the real director is the Holy Spirit. For the sake of convenience, I will use the term 'director', even though Ignatius might not be too happy.

126 David Fleming, *The Spiritual Exercises of Saint Ignatius – A Literal Translation and a Contemporary Reading,* p.5.

127 A very helpful article to read on this whole question of God's desires and my desires is Edward Kinerk, 'Eliciting Great Desires: Their Place in the Spirituality of the Society of Jesus' in *Studies in the Spirituality of Jesuits,* November 1984.

128 The fifth-century Athanasian Creed says, 'They that have done evil [will go] into everlasting fire.' The Fourth Lateran Council (1215) speaks of 'perpetual punishment with the devil'. The Second Council of Lyons (1270) asserts that those who die in mortal and original sin 'go down immediately to hell to be punished, however, with different punishments'. It is interesting that Vatican Council II does not mention hell explicitly.

129 'Pope Francis extols "gift of tears"', Megan Fincher in *National Catholic Reporter,* September 2013.

130 The *Anima Christi* has wrongly been attributed to Ignatius himself. Its provenance is disputed, but it is often ascribed to Pope John XXII, who reigned in Avignon from 1316 to 1334. A prayer book, belonging to Cardinal Peter de Luxembourg (+1387), containing the *Anima Christi* prayer, is to be found in the library at Avignon. Ignatius mentions the prayer as if the retreatant would already know it, though he does place the text itself at the very beginning of the Spiritual Exercises.

131 Julian of Norwich, *Revelations of Divine Love,* translated with an introduction by M. L. del Mastro, Image Books, New York, 1977, p.227.

132 ibid., p.226.

133 Decree 2 of General Congregation 34, The Institute of Jesuit Sources, St Louis, 1975.

134 The motto is taken from the writings of the Venerable Bede (673–735) when Bede is reflecting on Jesus' call of Matthew [Levi], the tax-collector (*Mt 9:9–13*).

135 The prayer is as follows: 'Eternal Lord of all things, I make my offering, with your favour and help. I make it in the presence of your infinite Goodness, and of your glorious Mother, and of all the holy men and women in your heavenly court. I wish and desire, and it is my deliberate decision, provided only that it is for your greater service and praise to imitate you in bearing all injuries and affronts, and any poverty, actual as well as spiritual, if your Most Holy Majesty desires to choose and receive me into such a life and state.' (98)

136 http://spckpublishing.co.uk/blog/spck-prayer/a-prayer-of-st-richard-of-chichester-1197-1253. This prayer was set to music for the popular musical *Godspell*.

137 It was Francis of Assisi who devised the first living crib in Greccio, Italy, in 1223. This was an attempt to discourage pilgrims from going to Bethlehem since the Holy Land was in the power of the Turks at the time.

138 Karl Rahner has an interesting comment on the idea of the 'two standards': 'St Ignatius presents us with the image of the two standards that are battling one another. This image has a pre-historical origin. It is constantly used in Scripture and tradition (for example Jerusalem–Babylon; the City of God and the City of Satan). But while tradition, at least since the time of St Augustine, draws a clear line between the fronts of the two kingdoms – the Church here and the kingdom of Satan over there – Ignatius emphasises the mutual penetration of both kingdoms. According to St Ignatius, there are no static front lines between the two, but only swift emissaries who are sent to all parts of the globe ... The kingdoms of Christ and Satan as described by St Ignatius both embrace the whole world. Lucifer also expands his power inside the Church, for there we find pride, greed for wealth, and power. The Church is also the Church of sinners and not just the Church of saints!' (*Spiritual Exercises,* Translated by Kenneth Baker SJ, Herder and Herder, New York, 1965, pp.170–71).

139 *Spiritual Exercises*, op. cit., p.177.
140 'Magis' means 'greater' and in the Ignatian context means 'that which gives greater glory and service to God'.
141 *Revelations of Divine Love,* op. cit., p.130.
142 Hans Urs von Balthasar, *Prayer*, Sheed & Ward, London, 1961, p.235.
143 In *The Way of Ignatius Loyola – Contemporary Approaches to the Spiritual Exercises*, edited by Philip Sheldrake, The Institute of Jesuit Sources, St Louis, 1999, pp.103–14.
144 Karl Rahner, *Spiritual Exercises,* op. cit., pp.218–22.
145 Joseph P. Cassidy SJ, 'Directing the Third Week', in *Review for Religious*, March–April 1990, pp.265–82.
146 Quoted in *Hearts on Fire – Praying with Jesuits,* ed. Michael Harter SJ, The Institute of Jesuit Sources, St Louis, 1993, p.73.
147 In *Review of Ignatian Spirituality*, xxx, 11/1999, p.48.
148 ibid., p.44.
149 See Michael Buckley SJ, 'The Contemplation to Attain Love', in *The Way Supplement* 24 (1975), pp.92–104.
150 'The heart is more devious than any other thing, perverse too: who can pierce its secrets?' (*Jer 17:9*).
151 'What the Spirit brings is very different: love, joy, peace, patience, kindness, goodness, trustfulness, gentleness and self-control' (*Gal 5:23*).
152 'An unspiritual person is one who does not accept anything of the Spirit of God: he sees it all as nonsense; it is beyond his understanding because it can only be understood by means of the Spirit. A spiritual man, on the other hand, is able to judge the value of everything, and his own value is not to be judged by other men' (*1 Cor 2:14–15*).
153 'It is not every spirit, my dear people, that you can trust; test them, to see if they come from God … You can tell the spirits that come from God by this: every spirit which acknowledges that Jesus Christ has come in the flesh is from God; but any spirit which does not say this of Jesus is not from God' (*1 Jn 4:1–3*).
154 A very helpful article on group discernment is 'Communal Discernment: Reflections on Experience', by John Carroll Futrell SJ in *Studies in the Spirituality of Jesuits*, November, 1972. Futrell suggests the following elements as being essential for authentic communal discernment: (1) Communion; (2) Communication [Common commitment]; (3) Trust; (4) Ability to listen; (5) Ability to recognise communal desolation.
155 *Ignatius of Loyola – Letters and Instructions,* op. cit., p.72.
156 ibid., p.8.
157 ibid.,p.19.
158 Michael Paul Gallagher, *Dive Deeper – The Human Poetry of Faith,* Darton, Longman & Todd, London, 2001, pp.78–93.
159 This meeting took place in Rome in October/November 2016. The meeting was composed of over 200 Jesuits from all over the world, gathered primarily to elect a new superior general.
160 Pope Francis is referring here to how Ignatius described himself in a letter from Rome, sent at the end of 1545 to Francis Borgia. Borgia was then Duke of Gandia, but was shortly to enter the Society of Jesus, in 1546. In this letter, Ignatius writes of himself, 'I am personally convinced regarding myself that before and after I am total obstacle. Because of this I feel spiritual happiness and joy in the Lord, inasmuch as I cannot attribute to myself even a semblance of good.'